W. B. YEATS
A CRITICAL INTRODUCTION

W. B. YEATS:
A CRITICAL
INTRODUCTION

Stan Smith

Barnes & Noble Books
Savage, Maryland

First published in the United States of America in 1990 by
Barnes & Noble Books
8705 Bollman Place
Savage, Maryland 20763

Library of Congress Cataloging-in-Publication Data
Smith. Stan, 1943–
    W. B. Yeats: a critical introduction/Stan Smith.
    p.   cm.
    ISBN 0–389–20902–3. – ISBN 0–389–20903–1 (pbk.)
    1. Yeats. W. B. (William Butler). 1865–1939 – Criticism and
Interpretation.   I. Title.
PR5907 S8 1990
821'.8 – dc20   90–32820
                                                                      CIP

For my students, past and present
'Nothing but a book . . .'

Contents

Acknowledgements   ix

1   Reading Yeats   1

2   Yeats: Biography and History   21
    2.1   Nationalism and the Anglo-Irish Tradition   21
    2.2   Family   24
    2.3   Golden Dawn and Celtic Twilight   27
    2.4   Maud Gonne and Theatre Business   34
    2.5   Independence Struggle and Civil War   40
    2.6   Maturity and Old Age   47

3   Yeats's Themes and Motifs   55
    3.1   How Themes are Embodied in a Poem   55
    3.2   Symbol and Image   58
    3.3   Falcon, Dove, Swan   61
    3.4   Imagination and Reality   63
    3.5   House and Tower   64
    3.6   The Anti-self or Mask   67
    3.7   Ireland, Byzantium and England   69
    3.8   Art, Aristocracy and Democracy   70
    3.9   Poet and People   73
    3.10 The Hero   77
    3.11 Beauty, Woman, Carnal Knowledge   81
    3.12 Philosophers and Dancers   84
    3.13 Folly and Madness   89
    3.14 Unrequited Love   91
    3.15 Age and 'Bodily Decrepitude'   98
    3.16 Terror and Apocalypse   100
    3.17 Yeats's Vision of History   104
    3.18 The Gyres   105
    3.19 Apollonian and Dionysian   109
    3.20 Repetition, Shadow, Archetype   111
    3.21 Troy, Leda, Helen, Adam   113
    3.22 Death and Rebirth   119

Contents

4 Style   122

5 Commentary: 'Meru'   153

   W. B. Yeats: a Life and Times   159

   A Guide to Further Reading   167
   1 Yeats's Texts   167
   2 Biographical, Historical and Cultural Contexts   169
   3 Critical Selections   170
   4 General Guides to the Poetry   171
   5 Studies of Particular Aspects   172

   Index of Poems Discussed   175
   Index of Names   178

Acknowledgements

Some sections of this book were first delivered as lectures in the Università degli Studi di Firenze during the spring and summer of 1987, and as a talk, 'The Folly That Men Do: Yeats and Women' at the British Institute, Florence.

I should like to thank my friends and colleagues in Florence for their kindness and hospitality, in particular Valerie Wainwright-Dari, Delma McDevitt and Tony Curran, Ornella de Zordo, Guido Clemente, Francesco Binni, Paolo and Susie Nello, Fred and Joanne Doll-Thweatt, and Rupert Hodson and the staff at the British Institute.

1

Reading Yeats

The aim of this study is to help the student at school and university to approach a difficult poet without being intimidated by him, and to write critically about his poetry without simply reproducing the ideas of established critics. I hope that in the process it will also give some sense of the vitality, urgency and contemporaneity of Yeats's work, and offer some new readings of the poetry.

The next three chapters provide a biographical and historical context for the work, an outline of its major themes, and an account of the key features of the poet's style. Besides providing the information needed to cope with any selection of the poetry, they aim to equip the student for an independent reading of that poetry by showing *how* these elements are combined in a poem, and *how* to approach them in any critical exercise.

By demonstrating how themes are embodied and events translated into *discourse*, the play of poetic language, the book offers a practical model for reading any poem, and introduces the reader to some of the technical vocabulary necessary for such a reading. It illustrates a range of stylistic features which one should look out for in critical analysis, revealing the way in which details of grammar and verbal texture become the sources of particular meaning and nuance. The fifth chapter offers a commentary on a short representative poem to illustrate how these elements can be brought together in a specific exercise of practical criticism. A brief chronology summarises the pertinent events of Yeats's life and works. The Guide to Further Reading offers an explanatory account of Yeats criticism which will help the student to find quickly and effectively the appropriate critical book for his or her project.

No poet in this century has shaped his work so directly out of reaction to the history of his times. Yeats's antithetical vision, his fascination with conflict, energy, turbulence and the *bodiliness* of being, his sense of poetry as a dramatic process, indicate how

1

closely bound up are the stylistic and the thematic dimensions of his art. As a poet of carnality and sexual love as much as of politics, Yeats is unexcelled. I would hope the reader will be encouraged by this book to see what an exciting writer he is, to perceive the contemporary relevance of his work, even in its more esoteric aspects, and to regard its study as less intimidating than it can sometimes seem.

W. B. Yeats is a writer's writer, and some of the most perceptive assessments of his work and his personality have come from fellow authors. His most eminent Irish successor, Seamus Heaney, has spoken of him as offering the practising writer 'an example of labour, effort, perseverance', because 'he reminds you that revision and slog work are what you may have to undergo if you seek the satisfaction of finish . . . if you have managed to do one kind of poem in your own way, you should cast off that way and face into another area of your experience until you have learned a new voice to fix and stay that area' ('Yeats as an Example?' in *Preoccupations: Selected Prose 1968–1978*, 1980).

Heaney emphasises one of the features of Yeats which I have tried to bring out in this introductory study – his restlessly self-transforming activity. Yeats's work changes enormously from early to late, as the biographical opening section indicates, and this is at once a change of style and of content. In fact, the two are inseparable, for Yeats works towards stylistic innovation by following the logic of a changed content, and his content is changed by experiments with form which generate their own new perceptions. As Heaney says, Yeats encourages us 'to experience a transfusion of energies from poetic forms them-selves, reveals how the challenge of a metre can extend the resources of the voice'. For 'deliberation', working over and over on a technical or thematic preoccupation until he has got it right, can itself become a form of 'inspiration'. Anyone who looks at the accounts of Yeats's various manuscript drafts by Jon Stallworthy or Curtis Bradford will see this. (The former is represented in Stallworthy's *Casebook*, the latter in Unterecker's *Twentieth Century Views* volume: see Guide to Further Reading.) It is hard to believe that the crude, stumbling drafts of 'Sailing to Byzantium', for example, can turn into the pellucid language of the opening stanza of the finished poem, which seems to

have come spontaneously, by an act of inspiration. The first
version of the opening stanza, according to Bradford, reads as
follows:

> This is no country for old men – if our Lord
> Smiles
> Is a smiling child upon his mother's knees
> And in the hills the old gods / those – I know now
> What names to call them by – still hunt and love
> There is still a love for those that can still sing
> All / For all the
> Forever sing the song that [. . .] you have sung. . . .

Etcetera. It is clear from the manuscripts that Yeats did not
usually start with a magical phrase or phrases from which the
poem organically grew. More often than not he started with an
idea, and then searched and struggled for the appropriate words
in which to embody it. 'Byzantium', for example, originated in
a plain prose instruction to himself, 'Subject for a poem':

> Describe Byzantium as it is in the system towards the end of
> the first Christian millenium. The worn ascetics on the walls
> contrasted with their splendour. A walking mummy. A
> spiritual refinement and perfection amid a rigid world. A sigh
> of wind – autumn leaves in the streets. The divine born amidst
> natural decay.

While we can learn much about the poems from looking at
these drafts, it should be clear that a prose paraphrase, even
when it is the poet's own programme notes for what he intends
to write, is no substitute for the finished poem. The poem is
not an original idea dressed up in poetic language. The ideas
here are too banal to merit further attention. There is no
substitute for the poem itself, for it is only the completed work
in its entirety that gives us its full meaning. This meaning
resides, not in pre-existing ideas, but in *the play of language* as
we read the poem.

One premise of this study is that, in looking at poetry, we do
not necessarily 'murder to dissect'. 'Taking a poem to pieces',
that barbarous phrase for critical analysis, would be an equally

barbarous activity if we then left the poem in fragments on the dissecting table. But we don't. On the contrary, critical analysis of the kind practised here is intended to show *how* a poem works, how it effects us in a particular way as the result of a skilled human activity, like the golden bird made by the Emperor's goldsmiths, which Yeats was not ashamed to use as a metaphor for his own art. In a culture dominated by 'organic' metaphors for creation, summed up by John Keats's beautiful but unhelpful aphorism, 'If poetry comes not as naturally as the leaves to a tree it had better not come at all', Yeats deliberately used a mechanical metaphor for poetry.

But this does not diminish poetry's stature. Rather it enhances it. For it shows that the 'magic' of poetry is not a matter of mystical inspiration from the supernatural, for all that Yeats might say of his spirit voices who came to give him 'metaphors for poetry'. Rather it is a matter of concerted human effort, using a range of talents to fashion words into something that functions as cunningly as a piece of carefully contrived precision clockwork. The 'witchcraft' is still there, but now we can see that it is a purely human craft that the poet practises. As Yeats wrote in 'Adam's Curse', the poet, like the beautiful woman, 'must labour to be beautiful'. Each alike must work hard to produce an effect that, to the reader or the observer, seems effortless:

> I said, 'A line will take us hours maybe;
> Yet if it does not seem a moment's thought,
> Our stitching and unstitching has been naught. . . .'
>
> I said, 'It's certain there is no fine thing
> Since Adam's fall but needs much labouring. . . .'

We should learn from this a greater respect for the inexhaustible possibilities of language itself, and admiration for the human mind that invented language and continuously forges new and unexpected possibilities from it. Critical analysis, then, aims to demonstrate in Heaney's words that poetry is 'intended', that it is 'part of the creative push of civilisation itself'.

It is frequently enough said that 'art' is universal, and 'life' particular. Yeats is a 'universal poet', like Shakespeare less for an age than for all time. This is a dangerous half-truth, and can lead us to misunderstand a poet's work in a way which finally diminishes it. There is a famous anecdote about the critic who misunderstood the lines of 'Among School Children',

> Plato thought nature but a spume that plays
> Upon a ghostly paradigm of things;
> Solider Aristotle played the taws
> Upon the bottom of a king of kings.

The phrase 'king of kings' misled the famous critic, for it is a term usually reserved in our culture for God, and the critic was writing at a period when the pursuit of Christian symbolism in poetry was a fashionable one. Added to this the critic, like most of his contemporaries, was convinced that poetry was concerned with great universals, with philosophical systems rather than the local events of history and politics, and he knew that in the Middle Ages the Ptolemaic *cosmology* – that is, an interpretation of how the universe, or cosmos, is constructed – had ruled the Christian world. This cosmology, derived ultimately from the fourth-century BC Greek philosopher Aristotle, saw the earth as the centre of the universe, with the sun and moon and stars revolving around it, moving in a series of crystalline spheres at various distances from the earth. Whereas the stars were fixed in these spheres, and the sun and moon moved round theirs in regular cycles, the planets wandered erratically over the heavens, causing disturbance in the world of men. An interpretation of Yeats's line was beginning to emerge, and the seal was set on this by the fact that the critic's American dictionary defined 'taws' as a game of marbles.

Marbles are of course rather like crystalline spheres, and they are placed in a series of circles around a central larger marble, the aim of the game being to disrupt them and if possible the central marble. A perfect image shaped itself for the critic. The unmoved marbles were the fixed stars, the moving marbles the wandering planets; the two cheeks of the bottom of the King of Kings were the twin crystalline spheres of moon and sun, upon which Aristotle played marbles by flicking the wandering planets at them. This the critic took as a complex image of Aristotle's

cosmology, as understood in the Middle Ages. In short, the
famous critic had lost his marbles.

A little clearer sense of history and of etymology might have
saved him his subsequent embarrassment. Aristotle, besides
being a philosopher, had been the teacher of the young boy
who was to grow up to become Alexander the Great. The
conqueror of many kingdoms in building up his empire, Alexander had himself deified as a King of Kings. Yet this mighty
monarch had once been a small boy at the mercy of his tutor. If
the critic had had a better dictionary, he would have learned
that in Ireland the taws is a leather strap for beating the bottoms
of ignorant or rebellious pupils. The lowly philosopher who,
unlike Plato, believed in the real existence of a material universe,
had 'first-hand' experience of the material world in the
classroom. Even a self-deified King of Kings was in reality no
more than an incompetent mortal, who could be chastised by
his humble teacher as the physical universe itself could be
submitted to the discipline of the philosopher's intellect.

The image is a highly appropriate one, for it emphasises the
issues of power that lie behind all knowledge and acts of
learning, a recurrent theme of Yeats's, contained for example in
the final question of 'Leda and the Swan', which records another
encounter of fleshly and divine, one that lies behind the swan
and child imagery of this poem: 'Did she put on his knowledge
with his power/Before the indifferent beak could let her drop?'.
'Among School Children', as its title reminds us, is set in a
classroom. If it raises highly philosophical questions about the
nature of the universe, art and order, it also raises questions
about the power of adults (teachers, parents, senators, nuns) to
shape the minds of the children in their charge – a power to
make them think in certain ways, hold certain beliefs, agree to
certain assumptions. This power, as Aristotle exemplifies, is
ultimately founded on physical violence.

The sophisticated critic's mistake actually illustrates the point
of Yeats's contrast between Aristotle and Plato. The critic, like
Plato, would rather create an elaborate system of 'ghostly
paradigms' of the universe, than interpret it in terms of the
sublunary material world of power relations in the state and
power relations in the class room. A little more knowledge about
Yeats's everyday Ireland, and a little less preoccupation with

abstract systems of philosophy, would have made the poem more readily comprehensible.

There is a crucial lesson here. Poetry is written by particular men and women in particular times and places, and it is read by equally particular people who live in a world of history, not of 'ghostly paradigms'. Understanding a text depends upon belonging to what the modern American critic Stanley Fish has called an *'interpretive [interpretative] community'*. This is a community of readers who share certain interpretations of words and ideas, perhaps unconscious assumptions about the way the world is constructed – in the end, a common cosmology. That is, they share precisely what the historian of ideas Thomas Kuhn has called a *paradigm* – a conceptual model for interpreting the world. Thus, in a Christian interpretative community, we will tend to assume that 'a king of kings' refers to Christ; whilst in Greece in the fourth century BC, we would have known that it was the title of Alexander the Great. Yeats, writing in twentieth-century Ireland about fourth-century Greece, sets up a tension between the two (and possibly) more interpretations of the phrase. (The fact that there are several possible candidates for the title is suggested by the use of the indefinite article 'a' rather than 'the' in referring to the king of kings.)

The larger paradigms shape our experience of literature as of everything else – whether the earth is flat or round; whether it was made by God on one day in 4004 BC or evolved as Darwin proposed over aeons of geological time; whether the best society is one based on individual private enterprise and competition or on public provision and co-operation; whether we should treat the weak and poor with contempt or protect them from their own weakness and poverty. These paradigms – and there are many more – can be instilled so early and so deeply that we are not even consciously aware of them as ideas at all. They are simply the way things are, identical with *common sense* itself. It is 'just commonsense', just agreed as in the natural order of things, that people should be allowed to make a profit out of the work of others; or that, if we are British, we should all be entitled to free medical treatment on the National Health, or, if we are Americans, that socialised medicine is a form of 'creeping Communism' – as much in the natural order of things as the certainty that the earth is round. Such deep-seated convictions, so deeply inculcated as to be largely unthinking, are what some modern critics would speak of as *ideology*, something which combines both conscious and unconscious assumptions about the nature of things.

Yeats is often spoken of as a highly ideological poet. But this is largely because he constantly makes explicit the assumptions and ideas that remain generally implicit in most people's accounts of the world. Added to this, many of Yeats's ideas go against the grain of our modern beliefs, and stand out more conspicuously as ideology than the ideas we take for granted.

He is, for example, aggressively hostile to the idea of democracy, which he sees as a levelling-down of excellence to the level of the lowest common denominator, rather than a sharing of power and responsibility between all members of a community. He is hostile to modern industry and commerce, which most of us assume to be the basis of social well-being and wealth. Both democracy and industry he associates with the English, who have imposed them upon an Ireland which believes (or *should* believe) in other things, in for example a feudal idea of *hierarchy*, where power is wielded by a small aristocracy over an unquestioning peasant people; and in an *organic society*, living close to and growing out the land, not dependent on the supposedly abstract, rootless values of the city and of capitalism. He believes that women should occupy a subordinate place in this society, and so on. An amusing and deliberately exaggerated view of Yeats's ideology has been given by the conservative American poet and critic Yvor Winters in *Forms of Discovery* (1967), writing of Yeats's fantasy of an ideal Ireland:

> Such a society would be essentially agrarian, with as few politicians and tradesmen as possible. The dominant class would be the landed gentry; the peasants would also be important, but would stay in their place; a fair sprinkling of beggars (some of them mad), of drunkards, and of priests would make the countryside more picturesque. The gentlemen should be violent and bitter, patrons of the arts, and the maintainers of order; they should be good horsemen, preferably reckless horsemen (if the two kinds may exist in one); and they should be fond of fishing. The ladies should be beautiful and charming, should be gracious hostesses

(although there is a place for more violent ladies . . .), should if possible be musicians, should drive men mad, love, marry, and produce children, should not be interested in ideas, and should ride horseback, preferably to hounds. So far as I can recollect, the ladies are not required to go fishing. What Yeats would have liked would have been a pseudo-eighteenth-century Ireland of his own imagining. He disliked the political and argumentative turmoil of revolutionary Ireland; he would scarcely have thought that the order which has emerged was sufficiently picturesque to produce poetry. (This essay is included in several anthologies; see Guide to Further Reading, sections 3 and 5.)

A poet's language, as we have seen with reference to 'taws', is not a timeless phenomenon, but has a history of its own. Words change their meaning over centuries, over decades, sometimes even over a few days. Yeats would not now be able to write, as he did in 'Lapis Lazuli', that 'Hamlet and Lear were gay', because the usage that this word has acquired since the 1970s would offer a startlingly new critical account of Shakespeare's tragic heroes. Yet when Yeats wrote this he was drawing very deliberately upon the philosophy of Friedrich Nietzsche, whose book *Fröhliche Wissenschaft* had been translated as 'The Gay Science' (another translation would call it 'The Joyous Knowledge'). The theme of Nietzsche's book is that which Yeats presents in many of his poems, including 'Among School Children'. Real knowledge is not acquired abstractly, in the schoolroom, under Aristotle's taws, but is learnt by lived, vital engagement, by a kind of joyous, excited involvement in what one is doing, as the Grecian goldsmith learns to work his metal only through hammering away at it, as the poet learns to use words only through wrestling with language, and as, one hopes, the reader of Yeats will learn something about language and about ideas by seeking to understand how Yeats's poems *work*.

It follows from this that anyone who wants to understand Yeats's poetry must have access to certain tools. Foremost of these is a good dictionary, the fullest possible – one that, like the *Oxford English Dictionary*, provides dates for the first usage of a particular meaning of a word, and certainly one that contains the Irish meaning of 'taws'. Also important is a mythological guidebook, for Greek and Celtic mythologies at least, and a reliable history of modern Ireland.

But the reader must also be prepared to handle these with some caution. I have attempted to indicate in the next chapter an idea of Irish history largely as Yeats perceived it, but with one or two necessary qualifications. The relations between Britain and Ireland are still, after seven hundred years, fraught and contentious. Some of the political movements which claim direct descent from Yeats's nationalist tradition are currently engaged in armed struggle with the British state, which they perceive as an occupying power. They are in turn perceived by that state, and by most of its citizens, including a majority in Ireland itself, as terrorists and criminals. Yeats's Protestant Irish community has changed beyond all recognition since his day. There remains hardly anything of the old Anglo-Irish Ascendancy. But the Protestant community of the North remains locked in religious and social confrontation with its Catholic neighbours.

'The Irish Problem' is a living instance of how powerful ideology is in the shaping of contemporary history – indeed, some critics would argue that to speak of it as 'The Irish Problem', rather than for example a problem of 'British Decolonisation', is itself an ideological construction. A lot depends on where you are standing – your *point of view* – when you make your definitions. As the modern English Marxist critic Terry Eagleton has written, in an issue of the Oxford journal *News from Nowhere* (1988):

The relations between poetry and politics may seem a little oblique in Macclesfield, but they are hardly so in Manila. You don't need a couple of stiff lecture courses, in the so-called third world, to press the case that culture and politics are profoundly interwoven; it's far easier to grasp the intricacies of discourse theory if somebody has been trying to rob you of your native speech. Ireland, it could be argued, emerged from third world status only in the middle decade of this century; and for the last few centuries 'culture' in Ireland has been a political battlefield, a bone of religious and class contention, an idiom in which questions of social identity and affiliation, political alliances and antagonisms, have been richly articulated.

Yeats himself has warned us what we have to avoid in an early letter he wrote to Katharine Tynan (1 May 1888) which remarks, with some exasperation, 'All these good English Home Rule people, how they do patronise Ireland and the Irish. As if we were some new sort of deserving poor for whom bazaars and such like should be got up. Yet they really are in earnest on this Home Rule question I think.'

I have tried to suggest briefly in the next chapter just how complex are the relations between religion, class and politics in Ireland. But what one should also bear in mind is that we are not talking here simply of *material relations* between people and peoples – how people actually stand in relation to each other in terms of what places they occupy in the power relations, the social, economic and cultural transactions between groups, classes and individuals. We are also talking about *ideological relations*, that is, about the ways in which people *perceive* and *interpret* and very often *misrepresent* to themselves and others their actual relations.

Yeats is very much a poet of conflicting Irish ideologies. That sense of drama, of dialectical activity, of conflict and struggle which I describe in his work, derives from his sense of these real political and economic struggles as also a struggle of ideologies – systems of belief and unconscious assumption – through which people try to understand their material relationships and history. Yeats himself spoke of this in 'A General Introduction for My Work' as a matter of the 'phantasmagorias' that we spin out of our lives. The 'phantasmagoria' expresses not the reality of our lives, but what we imagine, in a fantasy form or in the conflict of fantasies, to be their significance, and such competing phantasmagoria then become part of the reality.

Yeats shaped his best work out of a direct reaction to an ideological version of Irish history which was not only at odds with the British history books but also in conflict with the beliefs of many of his fellow Irishmen and women. As a member of the Anglo-Irish Protestant minority, Yeats's relation with that history was complex, and was further complicated by his own mythologising of it and of his personal relations with his friends

and lovers, and in particular the militant feminist and socialist
Maud Gonne. At the same time, Yeats throughout his life was
sensitive to the possibility that his own writings, from *Cathleen
ni Houlihan* through 'Easter 1916' to 'Parnell's Funeral' may have
had their own political effects, and agonised over this in a poem
such as 'The Man and the Echo':

> Did that play of mine send out
> Certain men the English shot?
> Did words of mine put too much strain
> On that woman's reeling brain?
> Could my spoken words have checked
> That whereby a house lay wrecked?

A biographical account of Yeats's life, then, also involves an
examination of the various 'phantasmagorias' he wove out of it,
whether in the early writings of the Celtic Twilight, with their
figures of the Irish Heroic Age, their delight in magic and the
supernatural, or in the head-on confrontations with the banal
realities of Dublin life of his maturity, what he called in 'The
Fascination of What's Difficult', 'the day's war with every knave
and dolt'. Yeats's pervasive vision of catastrophe may seem to
derive from those supernatural doctrines set out most systemati-
cally in his book *A Vision*. But it is not difficult to see in this
vision of *apocalypse*, of the end of an age in darkness and decay,
sombre echoes of the deepening crisis of Europe in the 1920s
and 1930s, as well as gloomy reflection on the decline of
the Protestant Ascendancy and the emergence of a new and
unwelcome Catholic, middle-class Ireland. Yeats's most immediate responses to the contemporary world are regularly reflected
in his mystical preoccupations, from the early Golden Dawn
Theosophy and the Celtic supernaturalism, through the interest
in Neo-Platonic and 'Hermetic', mystical thought, to the elaborate system of gyres and phases of *A Vision*. This study will
attempt to set out these ideas as succinctly as possible and show
how they relate to the larger dynamic of Yeats's poetry.

Louis MacNeice, a fellow Anglo-Irish poet from a Northern
Protestant background, summed up some of the familiar definitions of a contradictory Irishness in his early and still interesting study *The Poetry of W. B. Yeats* (reprinted in 1967). He

indicates how a sense of Ireland's historic conflicts can be ideologically defracted in ideas about the contrariness of Irish landscape and people:

> The Irish are born partisans [and] born puritans. . . . Their character could best be expressed in a set of antinomies. . . . We could say, for example: *The Irish are sentimental* (see any popular song book) but we could also say: *The Irish are unsentimental* (see [Bernard Shaw's] *John Bull's Other Island*). Or again: *The Irish genius is personal* (see Yeats passim and the popular English conception of the Irishman as a 'character') and *the Irish genius is impersonal* (see almost any translations of early Irish poetry). Or again: *The Irish are formal* (witness the conventions of the peasantry, the intricacies of Gaelic poetry, the political technique of Mr De Valera) and *The Irish are slapdash* (witness the way they ruin their houses). Or again: *Ireland is a land of Tradition* (think of the Irishman's notorious long memory) and *Ireland suffers from lack of Tradition* (see Yeats's well-founded strictures in *Dramatis Personae*). . . . The Irish dialectic is best, perhaps, resolved by a paradox: Ireland, like other countries, has obvious limitations; these limitations, if rightly treated, become assets. I would suggest therefore as a final antinomy this: *It is easy to be Irish; it is difficult to be Irish.*

MacNeice reveals the ideological at work here, in these irreconcilable descriptions each of which can be backed up with evidence. *Antithesis*, the balancing of often irreconcilable opposites, turns into *paradox*, which holds together two opposing possibilities in an impossible union, to become the literary figures of a political and ideological dilemma.

Paradox is a strategy for reconciling two *real*, historical incompatibilities at the level of *discourse*, in a *verbal* device. Yeats's 'antithetical vision' could be said to have its origins in an ideology of conflict resolved by paradox. When he delights in conflict and antinomy, one can see him using the possibilities of language, the fictioneer's ability to tell the truth while lying, to resolve dilemmas of allegiance and belief which he cannot resolve in life without opting unequivocally for one side or the other. Thus he creates *linguistic, dramatic* or *imaginary* resolutions of real and irresolvable dilemmas. As with MacNeice's formula, he uses poetry to have his cake and eat it.

MacNeice has other interesting things to say on Yeats's Irishness, which are relevant to an understanding of the present stage of Anglo-Irish relations as much as those of Yeats's day. He speaks, for example, of

> the clannish obsession with one's own family; the combination of an anarchist individualism with puritanical taboos and inhibitions; the half-envious contempt for England; the constant desire to show off; a sentimental attitude to Irish history; a callous indifference to those outside the gates; an identification of Ireland with the spirit and of England with crass materialism. Even now many Englishmen are unaware of the Irishman's contempt for England . . . the belief that the English are an inferior race.

We could do worse to begin to understand Yeats in his Irish and British contexts than to ask whether each of these ideological definitions of the Irish could not equally be applied, simply by changing round the names, to the English.

Yeats's politics are notoriously reactionary and right-wing, as we have seen. He comes close to fascism in his cult of Irish cultural purity and his admiration for the strong and masterful leadership of such figures as Italy's Mussolini, Spain's General Franco, and Ireland's O'Duffy. Yet one does not have to share these unpleasant views in order to admire and be moved by Yeats's poetry. Clearly, there is something more to Yeats's verse than the propagation of right-wing ideology. Various critics have addressed themselves to this problem – how can we enjoy this poetry when its values are inimical to most of those we believe in? – none more amusingly than the socialist George Orwell, who in 1943 linked Yeats's fascism to his other zany ideas (the essay is reprinted in *Collected Essays, Journalism and Letters*, vol. 2, 1968, and in several anthologies; see Guide to Further Reading, sections 3 and 5):

> How do Yeats' political ideas link up with his leaning towards occultism? It is not clear at first glance why hatred of democracy and a tendency to believe in crystal-gazing should go together

. . . but it is possible to make two guesses. To begin with, the theory that civilisation moves in recurring cycles is one way out for people who hate the concept of human equality. If it is true that 'all this', or something like it, 'has happened before', then science and the modern world are debunked at one stroke and progress becomes for ever impossible. It does not matter if the lower orders are getting above themselves, for, after all, we shall soon be returning to an age of tyranny. . . . If the universe is moving round on a wheel, the future must be foreseeable, perhaps even in some detail. It is merely a question of discovering the laws of its motion, as the early astronomers discovered the solar year. Believe that, and it becomes difficult not to believe in astrology or some similar system. . . . Secondly, the very concept of occultism carries with it the idea that knowledge must be a secret thing, limited to a small circle of initiates. But the same idea is integral to Fascism. Those who dread the prospect of universal suffrage, popular education, freedom of thought, emancipation of women, will start off with a predilection towards secret cults. There is another link between Fascism and magic in the profound hostility of both to the Christian ethical code.

The poet W. H. Auden, writing four years earlier, when he was still close to communism, is more generous to Yeats, trying to separate out Yeats's reactionary ideas from what Auden saw as the 'progressive' side of his nationalism and anti-capitalism. Yeats was opposed to capitalism and imperialism, Auden argued in 'The Public v. the Late Mr William Butler Yeats' in *Partisan Review* in 1939 (reprinted in several anthologies; see Guide to Further Reading, sections 3 and 5). In a small, backward, largely agrarian country such positive beliefs could easily be deflected into a negative mode:

The most obvious social fact of the last forty years is the failure of liberal capitalist democracy. . . . By denying the social nature of personality, and by ignoring the social power of money, it has created the most impersonal, the most mechanical, and the most unequal civilisation the world has ever seen. . . . From first to last [Yeats's poems] express a sustained protest against the social atomisation caused by

industrialism, and both in their ideas and their language a
constant struggle to overcome it. The fairies and heroes of the
early work were an attempt to find through folk tradition a
binding force of society; and the doctrine of Anima Mundi
found in the later poems is the same thing, in a more
developed form, which has left purely local peculiarities
behind, in favour of something that the deceased hoped was
universal; in other words, he was working for a world religion.
A purely religious solution may be unworkable, but the search
for it is, at least, the result of a true perception of a social evil.
Again, the virtues that [he] praised in the peasantry and
aristocracy, and the vices he blamed in the commercial classes
were real virtues and vices. To create a united and just society
where the former are fostered and the latter cured is the task
of the politician, not the poet.

But, Auden goes on, Yeats's style enters into conflict with his
ideas. There is a kind of dialectical tension between what his
content says and what his form tells us:

> However false or undemocratic his ideas, his diction shows a
> continuous evolution toward what one might call the true
> democratic style. The social virtues of a real democracy are
> brotherhood and intelligence, and the parallel linguistic virtues
> are strength and clarity, virtues which appear even more
> clearly through successive volumes. . . . The diction of *The
> Winding Stair* is the diction of a just man, and it is for this
> reason that just men will always recognise the author as a
> master.

What we have to be aware of is a verse that gives out many
more and contradictory messages than those that the author
consciously intends. A poem, that is, is *polysemic*: it contains
many messages, and it cannot be reduced to one simple idea
which we can then offer in a paraphrase, thereby doing away
with the need for the poem itself. Rather, the poem exists simply
as the putative total of all the readings we can make of it,
holding together a collection of different and often irreconcilable
points of view, some of them personal to the poet and others
emerging from the *complexity* and *ambiguity* of the language

itself. In a richer sense than is usually intended, then, Yeats's poetry is *dialectical*, a drama of contending views. Indeed, it could be said more accurately that it is incorrigibly *plural*, containing as many possibilities of interpretation as there are interpretative communities to elicit them. I shall explore some aspects of this in the next three sections.

Auden's reclamation of Yeats for a left-wing democratic tradition is not just an exercise in self-delusion: it illustrates Stanley Fish's argument that there is no stable meaning to a poem but rather a theoretically infinite set of possible interpretations. This means, at its most practical, that the student must not be browbeaten into believing that there is only *one* authentic interpretation of a poem, which has been arrived at already by some established critic or another. Rather, a poem's meaning is always open-ended and potential, capable of being renegotiated by a critic persuasive enough to produce a new reading of which he or she can convince us. Indeed, a central tenet of recent and currently widely influential *deconstructive theories* of literature is that we can always begin over again, finding some new instability and disturbance in the poem which unsettles the fixed, traditional consensus of interpretations. In considering how a poem carries its ideology, we have to see how it transforms it, and this means looking not only at the overt themes but at how those themes are *embodied* in the poetry. It is with this in view that I have emphasised in the third chapter the linguistic processes by which themes, abstract ideas, become concrete images and events in the body of Yeats's verse.

A major principle of literary criticism since T. S. Eliot published his widely influential essay 'Tradition and the Individual Talent' in 1919 is the idea of the *impersonality* of poetry. This does not mean that the poet assumes a pose that is aloof, cold and impersonal, though in Yeats this is often the case. Rather it means that a poem exists in the same way as a marble statue (a common image in Yeats) or as the clockwork bird of the Byzantium poems. That is, it exists independently of the personality of its author. It does not express his emotions and beliefs. Instead, it takes those passing emotions and beliefs, and the language in which they are embodied, as the raw material of poetry, making of them 'monuments of unageing intellect' in the same way that the sculptor uses his raw materials to create statues which, in the words of 'Among School Children', 'keep a marble or a bronze repose'.

This is what Yeats means when he speaks, in 'A General Introduction for My Work', of making a collective 'phantasmagoria' out of the private experiences of the poet, so that 'he is more type than man, more passion than type'. The person who appears to speak to us directly from the poem, 'even when the poem seems most himself . . . is never the bundle of accident and incoherence that sits down to breakfast; he has been reborn as an idea, something intended, complete' (see Chapter 3.6). When we look, say, at Rembrandt's self-portraits, we are not interested in them primarily for what they tell us about Rembrandt himself, the man who sat down to breakfast before painting them. Rather we look at them as *images* of a human being who seems to be in front of us, in the present, and yet who also seems to gaze back at us over three centuries in which Rembrandt the painter and Rembrandt the sitter has long since turned to dust.

The art resides, that is, in the perpetual present tense of a 'phantasmagoria', in the play of light, line and colour, of imagined mass and depth in what is in reality a flat, two-dimensional canvas. In the same way, the 'Yeats' that speaks to us as if directly from the poem is no more than a play of language, of the sound, meaning and texture of words, what the modern critic would call a *discursive practice* – a *play of discourse* which produces the *effect*, in us, of hearing Willy Yeats speak. This emphasis on poetry as the *production of effects* in the reader carries with it, too, a sense of our responsibility as readers. For in reading a poem we are not simply passively consuming an already created object. Rather we are engaged in actively recreating it, giving it a new life and meaning in our understanding of it. Such an insight, which is already there in Yeats's aesthetics, has led to a whole school of modern critical thought known as *reader-response* or, in a phrase popularised by Stanley Fish, *reception theory*. But this last term is misleading because it does not draw attention to the active role of the reader in *reproducing* the poem, not simply passively *receiving* it. Every act of reading is itself a creative act, though it may be a more or less adequate act of creation.

The personal life of a poet and his or her times is transmuted into the impersonality of discourse, the 'golden bird or golden handiwork' of the Byzantium poems, only so that it can return to the personal sphere in our own re-readings. In reading a poem, like the drowsy emperor and the lords and ladies of Byzantium listening to that clockwork bird, we are allowing it to sing once again, out of 'the artifice of eternity', of the world of historical time, 'Of what is past, or passing, or to come'.

T. S. Eliot, in a magisterial essay in *On Poetry and Poets* (1957), has written of Yeats's impersonality as that of a poet intensely preoccupied with the personal, who,

> out of intense and personal experience, is able to express a general truth; retaining all the particularity of his experience, to make of it a general symbol. And the strange thing is that Yeats, having been a great craftsman in the first kind [of impersonality], became a great poet in the second. It is not that he became a different man, for . . . one feels sure that the intense experience of youth had been lived through – and indeed, without this early experience he could never have attained anything of the wisdom which appears in his later writing.

Such an ability to transform the personal into the impersonal, into a 'phantasmagoria', is for Eliot inseparable from Yeats's unique and intimate relationship to the history of his times:

> There are some poets whose poetry can be considered more or less in isolation, for experience and delight. There are others whose poetry, though giving equally experience and delight, has a larger historical importance. Yeats was one of the latter; he was one of those few whose history is the history of their own time, who are part of the consciousness of an age which cannot be understood without them.

What I hope to suggest in the rest of this book is the interdependence of Yeats's personal and public poses. Each informs the other. Every love poem carries the secret signature of a political and cultural origin. Each public poem is charged with a surplus of emotion which has its resources in the private sphere. In a phrase much used in contemporary feminist writing, for Yeats 'the personal is political'. It is this which makes him, in Eliot's words, 'a unique and especially interesting poet', a poet for our own time.

2
Yeats: Biography and History

2.1 NATIONALISM AND THE ANGLO-IRISH TRADITION

The biography of William Butler Yeats is inseparable from the history of Irish nationalism. Both in turn provide major themes for his poetry. Born in Dublin on 13 June 1865 into a professional middle-class family, Yeats inherited as his birthright what Stephen Gwynne was to describe as the condition of being 'spiritually hyphenated without knowing it'. 'Spiritual hyphenation' was the dilemma of the Anglo-Irish Protestant minority to which both poets belonged, descendants largely of English, Scots or Huguenot stock settled in the country in the wake of Elizabeth I's and Cromwell's bloody reconquests of Ireland in the sixteenth and seventeenth centuries. Born and bred in the country for three hundred years, feeling itself Irish as much as British, the Protestant minority nevertheless had many of the characteristics of a colonial, settler establishment, and remained largely aloof from the Catholic, originally Gaelic-speaking native population.

The latter had lost most of its land to the Anglo-Irish aristocracy, known as 'the Ascendancy', which drew its livelihood largely from rents from its estates and (when not absentee landlords in Dublin or London) was based in the great country houses celebrated in poems such as 'Ancestral Houses'. The Ascendancy found its careers in the higher echelons of the military, colonial and civil services. Lady Augusta Gregory, for example, Yeats's patron and friend, whose Coole Park is evoked in several of his poems, was the widow of the Governor of Ceylon, and her son Robert died a major in the British Air Force. At the same time, particularly in the North, a class of small landowning Protestant farmers had prospered. Both these classes were sustained by the trading and professional strata from which Yeats's own family derived. When, therefore, he speaks in 'The Tower' of inheriting from his forbears 'the pride of people that were/Bound neither to Cause nor to State,/Neither to slaves that were spat on,/Nor to the tyrants that spat', he is not being completely honest.

It was important to Yeats to establish the Protestant strand in Irish nationalism. It mattered, for example, that his great-grandfather, the Rev. John Yeats, Rector of Drumcliff in Co. Sligo, was, as he says in 'Introductory Rhymes', 'Robert Emmet's friend, / A hundred-year old memory to the poor'. The Protestant Emmet was executed in 1803 for leading a rebellion against British rule, and John Yeats was himself imprisoned briefly under suspicion of supporting the rebellion. The Protestant tradition also, in the eighteenth century, supplied several of Yeats's literary heroes: the political theorist Edmund Burke, the satirist Jonathan Swift, poet and playwright Oliver Goldsmith, and the philosopher Bishop Berkeley, are all celebrated in various poems. In Yeats's own day the tradition was to provide in Charles Stewart Parnell, the leader of the Irish Party at Westminster, the one statesman who could have led Ireland to united independence. But Parnell was brought down by a divorce which scandalised a people that, even as it threw off the yoke of the British imperial state, was unable to break free from the power of the Church of Rome.

It is true that many of the leaders of the nationalist cause, from Emmet and Wolfe Tone, leader of the United Irishmen in the 1798 Rebellion, through to Parnell were drawn from the Protestant minority. But there is no doubt that the 'pride' of which Yeats speaks was underwritten by real economic, legal, political and religious privileges, privileges which bound it to the 'tyrants that spat'. The rebellion of 1798, which brought together Catholics and Protestants inspired by the American and French Revolutions, led only to suppression and the dissolution of the Irish Parliament in the Act of Union with Britain in 1800. The efforts of the eighteenth-century statesmen Yeats invokes in 'The Tower', Edmund Burke and Henry Grattan, to achieve better terms of trade for Ireland, improve tax and land rights for the peasantry, and secure a limited franchise and freedom of worship for Catholics, all came to nothing. In the end, such men remained representatives of the landowning interest from which they came, unable really to understand or share in the assumptions of the dispossessed and disfranchised Catholic majority. Indeed, Yeats admired Burke primarily for his conservative doctrine of the state as an organic whole which would only be damaged by the tinkerings of reformers – that 'haughtier-headed Burke who proved the state a tree' spoken of in 'Blood and the Moon', who had opposed the French Revolution.

It was not until the leadership of the Catholic Daniel O'Connell that Catholic Emancipation was secured, in 1829. But Yeats despised O'Connell, dismissing him in 'Parnell's Funeral' as 'the Great Comedian', and remarking, on his American lecture tour in 1904, that 'He taught the people to lay aside the pike and musket, the song and the story, and to do their work now by wheedling and now by bullying. He won certain necessary laws for Ireland. . . . He was the successful politician, but it was the unsuccessful Emmet who has given her patriots.' More to Yeats's taste was the militancy of the Young Ireland movement, which under the pressure of the Great Famine of the 1840s rejected O'Connell's constitutionalism in favour of 'physical force', and attempted an insurrection in 1848, a year of revolutions throughout Europe. Drawn largely from the urban professional classes, many of them Protestants, the Young Irelanders left behind a residue of cultural nationalism, 'song and story', which was to set an example for the young Yeats.

Famine and emigration embittered the new generations of nationalists, and Land Acts of 1870 and 1881 which partially alleviated the lot of the peasantry offered too little too late. The upsurge of the 'Home Rule' movement in the second half of the century was based largely in the Catholic peasantry and newly emergent Catholic middle class, and was accompanied by a growing campaign to resurrect Gaelic. The Irish Republican Brotherhood (IRB, or 'Fenians', after the warriors of the ancient hero Finn McCool) was founded in 1858 to seek independence by 'physical force' (the Young Ireland slogan). This was seven years before Yeats's birth. The year his family moved to London, 1867, a Fenian Rising was put down with considerable violence. In 1879, a year before the family returned to Ireland, the Irish Land League was founded, on the initiative of Parnell and

Michael Davitt, with its brutally effective answer to the land problem: boycott and burn out the landlords.

In 1882, the murder in Phoenix Park, Dublin, of two eminent politicians led to the suppression of the League. By 1887, however, when the family returned once more to London, Gladstone's Liberal government had come to rely on Parnell's Irish Party for support, and the First Home Rule Bill, defeated in Parliament in 1886, led to sectarian rioting in the streets of Belfast. Increasingly the Protestant minority identified with the idea of continued union with Britain ('Unionism'). This led to a further polarisation. Protestants came to be distrusted by the nationalist movement, even though many, including most of Yeats's acquaintances and friends, remained advocates of Home Rule. As a young man, Yeats himself was a member of the IRB.

Yeats despised what he saw as the hypocritical religiosity of the Catholic lower-middle classes who had turned against Parnell, and indicts them in several poems. By contrast he celebrates the heroic solitude of men such as Parnell and Grattan, who seemed to represent an alternative, aristocratic tradition with which he could identify. The clash between these two forces in Irish history creates one of the most powerful tensions in his poetry, and the need to synthesise such warring antitheses into a unity became his strongest literary and political impulse.

2.2   FAMILY

For Yeats, this complex history of spiritual hyphenation was compounded by the move two years after his birth to London, where the family lived for the next fourteen years, returning once again in 1887 after seven years in Dublin. The movement backwards and forwards was to set the pattern for Yeats's later life. The young Yeats thus derived much of his initial sense of Ireland from the frequent visits to his mother's family, the Pollexfens, prosperous landowners in Sligo in the rural West of Ireland, while his father remained in London, pursuing his career as a portrait painter. The contrast between the mundane world of school and suburb associated with Hammersmith and Chiswick, and the magical realm of the West, lies at the heart of many of Yeats's later dichotomies.

His father, John Butler Yeats, derived from a family of merchants and small landowners which by the beginning of the nineteenth century had moved into the professions and, in particular, the Church of Ireland. This, the established, state-supported church, was the religion of the Ascendancy, distinguished on the one hand from the Roman Catholicism of the native peasantry, and on the other from the Presbyterian and other low church sects of tradesman and working-class settlers. An artist and a free thinker, J. B. Yeats early rejected the religion of his own father, the Rev. William Butler Yeats, the Rector of Tullyish in Co. Down, and his son in turn inherited his irreligious and at times anti-clerical bent (something revealed at its clearest in the 'Crazy Jane' poems).

Nevertheless, in his poetry, Yeats was to make much of his ancestry on both sides of the family. He turns repeatedly in the poems to those 'old fathers' of whom he asks pardon in 1914 in the 'Introductory Rhymes' to *Responsibilities*, and judgement in 1938 in 'Are You Content?' In both poems it is the supposedly romantic aspects of these ancestors which appeal to him, though he manages to invest even the occupation of merchant with glamour by associating it with smuggling in the one and distinguishing it from the vulgar trade of 'huckster' in the other. He speaks in the first poem of ancestors who supported the Dutch William of Orange against the Catholic James II at the Battle of the Boyne in 1690:

> Merchant and scholar who have left me blood
> That has not passed through any huckster's loin,
> Soldiers that gave, whatever die was cast:
> A Butler or an Armstrong that withstood
> Beside the brackish waters of the Boyne
> James and his Irish when the Dutchman crossed. . . .

While in the second he speaks of:

> That red-headed rector in County Down,
> A good man on a horse,
> Sandymount Corbets, that notable man
> Old William Pollexfen,

> The smuggler Middleton, Butlers far back,
> Half legendary men.

In another poem, 'Under Saturn', he speaks more self-critically of going on a 'fantastic ride', goaded 'By childish memories of an old cross Pollexfen / And of a Middleton . . . , / And of a red-haired Yeats whose looks . . . seem like a vivid memory'. It is certainly true that for Yeats what he calls these 'Half legendary men' become part of his own personal mythology, part of that 'phantasmagoria' which, he says elsewhere, a poet creates out of his life and times. He was to do the same thing with his contemporaries – lovers, friends and enemies alike – forging what 'The Municipal Gallery Revisited' calls 'an Ireland / The poets have imagined, terrible and gay'. Thus Yeats's family, friends and foes are not merely part of the background of his poetry. They are right at its centre, the characters who make up his imaginative world as much as the dwellers of Wessex inhabit Hardy's novels.

Yeats's ancestors on both sides were drawn mainly from seventeenth-century settlers. As merchants, lawyers, clerics, they were nowhere near so grand as the Ascendancy they served. On his father's side, however, Yeats could trace descent from older settler stock. His great-great grandfather had married Mary Butler, thus bringing into the family both landed property and a name which linked them with one of the oldest and most powerful Ascendancy families, settled there in the twelfth century. In making much of this connection in his verse Yeats was merely perpetuating a family snobbery, for the middle name 'Butler' was handed down from father to son as a token of this superior inheritance. In the original version of 'Introductory Rhymes' Yeats had romantically imagined his Butler ancestors fighting at the Battle of the Boyne in 1690 on the side of the Catholic James II, rather than for the Protestant William of Orange ('the Dutchman', whose victory, restoring British rule in Ireland, is still today celebrated by the Orange Orders of Ulster). Yeats corrected this in later versions, but the change from imaginary to real allegiance does not seem to have altered his assessment of his ancestors as authentically Irish, not least in their readiness (like Major Robert Gregory in 'An Irish Airman

Foresees his Death') to die for a cause without counting the cost or asking whether they really believed in it.

In 1919 Yeats recalled, in the essay 'If I Were Four-and-Twenty', that in his early twenties (that is, in the last years of the 1880s), a sentence seemed to form insistently in his head: 'Hammer your thoughts into unity'. At the time, he records,

> I had three interests; interest in a form of literature, in a form of philosophy, and a belief in nationality. None of these seemed to have anything to do with the other, but gradually my love of literature and my belief in nationality came together. Then for years I said to myself that these two had nothing to do with my form of philosophy. . . . Now all three are, I think, one, or rather all three are a discrete expression of a single conviction.

Forging these connections was to be a lifetime's work.

2.3 GOLDEN DAWN AND CELTIC TWILIGHT

Yeats's schooldays were undistinguished. He was regarded as a dreamer and a waster, and he never went to university, though there was talk in 1911, when he was already a famous literary figure, of his succeeding Edward Dowden as Professor of Literature at Trinity College, Dublin. Initially it looked as if Yeats might follow his father, and he was registered in 1884–5 as a student at the Metropolitan School of Art in Dublin. Surviving pastel sketches suggest that he had little artistic talent, and are derivative of the Pre-Raphaelites whose poetry, also, was to influence his own early writing. It was here that he met the nationalist mystic and writer George Russell, who published under the pseudonym 'AE', and it was from him that he derived his first encouragement to link his interest in the occult to a political as well as an artistic vision. For AE, the ancient Irish were a visionary people, and their spirit world linked with that of Buddhism and the Theosophy which had become fashionable in the airy-fairy circles in which the two moved. The conjunction was to be a crucial one in Yeats's development.

In revolt against a materialistic age, but out of sympathy with conventional Christianity, the young Yeats was attracted to the various mysticisms and mystical societies that floated around the *fin de siècle* (the 'end of the century'). He found here a concern with magic and ritual, 'astral bodies', séances and occult ceremonies, which appealed to his anti-scientific bent. At the age of twenty he was a founder member of the Dublin Hermetic Society, a secret order devoted to the study of oriental religions and the writings supposedly by the ancient Graeco-Egyptian sage Hermes Trismegistus. Two years later, in 1887, he joined the London Lodge of the Theosophists, a sect of spiritualists based on the 'revelations' of the charismatic charlatan Madame Blavatsky. Expelled in 1890 for favouring a critical though sympathetic approach to the evidence for supernatural phenomena, Yeats devoted his time more and more to the Hermetic Students of the Golden Dawn, which he had recently joined. In the poem 'All Souls' Night', written in 1920, he attempts to call up the ghosts of some of the people he encountered here, in particular William Thomas Horton and MacGregor Mathers, founder members of the Order.

The Golden Dawn was dedicated to exploring the mystical doctrines of the Kabbala, the Jewish tradition of arcane wisdom and magic. The secret books of the Kabbala contained much that had spilled over from Neo-Platonic thought, particularly in the idea that the universe is made up of a series of overflows from a pure primal source, the spiritual becoming coarser and coarser in each stage of the descent until it becomes matter, the crudest embodiment of spirit. This metaphor lies behind much of Yeats's thought. It is the basis, for example, of the ideas he was later to incorporate in his philosophy of history, published first in 1925, *A Vision*, and such poems as 'The Phases of the Moon' and 'Chosen'. It lies behind the image of the overflowing fountain at the beginning of 'Ancestral Houses' as well as being explicitly referred to in 'A Dialogue of Self and Soul' as the primal 'fullness' of being which 'overflows / And falls into the basin of the mind'.

The Golden Dawn gave Yeats much of his most effective imagery, imagery reworked again and again throughout his life. The cleansing 'holy fire' of, for example, the 'Byzantium' poems, like that flame which consumes the entire combustible world in 'In Memory of Major Robert Gregory' or a doomed Troy in innumerable poems, has its origins here, in the idea of a mystical blaze in which the adept is purged of impurities and returns to the source. In one of his last poems, 'The Circus Animals' Desertion', Yeats speaks of 'masterful images' which 'grew in pure mind' but began 'In the foul rag and bone shop of the heart'. These images (those of art and occult religion alike, which give mastery over the world of nature) are attained only by climbing the ladder which 'ascends to Heaven'. In the 'Dialogue of Self and Soul' the 'steep ascent' is up that 'winding stair' which for Yeats is symbolically embodied in the stair of his Norman Tower, the setting for many poems, and the title of one of his most powerful volumes. But even the ordinary ladders Michael Angelo (Yeats's spelling of Michelangelo) has to climb to paint the Sistine Chapel ceiling, in 'The Long-Legged Fly' or 'Under Ben Bulben', figure forth the same idea. To reach 'Profane perfection of mankind', the latter poem suggests, artist or adept has to undergo a secret discipline which purges his sensual body of impurities and 'completes his partial mind', in order to 'Bring the soul of man to God'.

The dawn, as a site of transition and change, was itself to be one of Yeats's recurring images, yet it is a completely traditional one. More esoteric perhaps is the unexpected conjunction in his early poetry of two other traditional symbols, the Rose and the Cross, particularly in the poems from *The Rose* and *Crossways*. 'To the Rose upon the Rood of Time', for example, has the rose of life, love and beauty crucified upon the cross of time. The 'Golden Dawn' was a 'Rosicrucian' society, following mystical doctrines supposedly initiated in the fifteenth century by Christian Rosenkreutz ('Our Father Rosicross' of 'The Mountain Tomb'). For Yeats, the mystic Rose can be interchangeably the spirit, beauty, and the woman he met and fell in love with in 1889, who was to dominate his life and poetry for the next half-century: Maud Gonne. It can even be, in poems such as 'To Ireland in the Coming Times', Ireland herself, martyred by a violent history.

Yet, in so far as these early poems have any charm, it is in their ethereal, 'wavering' cadences, and in their sense of a mysterious meaning hinted at and withheld. To try to explain the symbols is to destroy this fragile power, by reducing the vague and nebulously symbolic to a spuriously precise, mechanical and systematic allegory – the very opposite of all Yeats was aiming for.

The early poetry is that of a competent minor poet, able to reproduce the langorous rhythms and world-weary attitudes of the period that starts in the late 1880s, often called 'the Decadence', or the *fin de siècle*, on the assumption that the dying years of a century are peculiarly prone to such moods, shifting between apocalyptic hopes of a second coming or revolution, and 'decadent' proclamations that nothing really matters and therefore everything is allowed. Such attitudes are those of the 'sick children of the world' referred to in 'The Song of the Happy Shepherd', one of Yeats's earliest published poems.

The woods of Arcady (the imaginary Greek realm of carefree pastoral content) are now dead, the Shepherd tells us, and a world which once 'fed' on dreaming (the suggestion is that this was a life-giving thing) has now turned to 'Grey Truth' for its 'painted toy'. The 1880s and 90s were a period of artistic reaction against the growing dominance of scientific and utilitarian thinking in all areas of life, brought about by the successes of industrial and commercial capitalism on a global scale, which had led to what Yeats's generation saw as the mechanisation of social life, the debasement of culture, and the growth of a democracy of the lowest common denominator. 'Grey Truth' here is Yeats's phrase for such a frame of mind, which rejects all things of the spirit as 'mere dreams', and believes that only 'facts' are real (and 'facts' usually have something to do with making money). Such an attitude he summed up at the end of his life as the product of three centuries of belief in 'progress' (a word and an idea he despised), in his 'Introduction to the Oxford Book of Modern Verse':

When my generation denounced scientific humanitarian preoccupation, psychological curiosity, rhetoric, we had not found what ailed Victorian literature. . . . The mischief began at the end of the seventeenth century when man became passive before a mechanised nature. . . . Or I may dismiss all that ancient history and say it began when Stendhal described a masterpiece as a 'mirror dawdling down a lane'. (A. N. Jeffares (ed.), *W. B. Yeats: Selected Criticism and Prose* (1980), hereafter referred to as C.)

The 'Song' suggests that 'Grey Truth', a concern with facts and practicalities, is more idle and less 'real' than dreaming. Against the supposedly 'realistic' concerns of a world obsessed by scientific and industrial 'progress', Yeats sets the power of language, apparently ephemeral, frail, easily dismissed, yet outliving the 'warring kings' of old time. They, after all, now only survive as 'some entangled story' read by 'the stammering schoolboy'. The world itself, he says, may be 'Only a sudden flaming word, / In clanging space a moment heard, / Troubling the endless reverie.' The best gloss on this is provided by the Introduction to *The Symbolist Movement in Literature* (1899), dedicated to Yeats by his friend Arthur Symons: 'Symbolism began with the first words uttered by the first man, as he named every living thing; or before them, in heaven when God named the world into being'. 'Reverie' is a characteristic word of the period, though Yeats carries it right through to his last poems as a metaphor for an alternative kind of knowledge to that of science, and in 'A Bronze Head' he speaks caustically of 'Heroic reverie mocked by fool and knave'.

Though the shepherd ends by urging us to 'Dream, dream, for this is also sooth', there seems little in his song to suggest that he is truly happy, for he departs to sing 'mirthful songs' only over the grave of some 'hapless faun'. He seems no more content in fact than 'The Sad Shepherd'. Even his advice to find comfort in telling our story to 'Some twisted, echo-harbouring shell' on the seashore seems ineffectual. The 'sad shepherd' seems to have followed the advice, but to no avail, for all he sings is simply changed into 'inarticulate moan'. In the second poem, only the stars on 'their pale thrones . . . / Among themselves laugh on and sing alway'. But this is no comfort to the shepherd. The two poems together present not contrasting moods but two variations on the same world-weariness, one arbitrarily labelled 'happy' and the other 'sad'. It is a characteristic mood, accompanied in poem after poem of this period by an imagery of stars and clouds, woods, waves and waters, moonlight and twilight, reiterating, in the words of the refrain to 'The Stolen Child' that 'the world's more full of weeping than you can understand'. 'The White Birds' is a typical, and highly effective, instance of such verse, with its simple, almost banal imagery expressed in lingering, wavering rhythms full of repetition and return, vague exclamations and long dying cadences:

> I would that we were, my beloved, white birds on the foam
>   of the sea!
> We tire of the flame of the meteor, before it can fade and
>   flee;
> And the flame of the blue star of twilight, hung low on the
>   rim of the sky,
> Has awaked in our hearts, my beloved, a sadness that may
>   not die.
>
> A weariness comes from those dreamers, dew-dabbled, the
>   lily and rose;
> Ah, dream not of them, my beloved, the flame of the meteor
>   that goes,
> Or the flame of the blue star that lingers hung low in the fall
>   of the dew:
> For I would we were changed to white birds on the wandering
>   foam: I and you!
>
> I am haunted by numberless islands, and many a Danaan
>   shore,
> Where Time would surely forget us, and Sorrow come near
>   us no more;
> Soon far from the rose and the lily and fret of the flames
>   would we be,
> Were we only white birds, my beloved, buoyed out on the
>   foam of the sea!

Because of their combination of 'Decadent' attitudes and Irish
themes, volumes such as *The Wind Among the Reeds* (1899) and
In the Seven Woods (1904) are often spoken of as the poetry of
'the Celtic Twilight'.

This is a verse full of pale shadowy figures from Celtic myth:
'Fergus and the Druid', 'Cuchulain Fights with the Sea'. Niamh
in 'The Hosting of the Sidhe' calls us to 'empty [our] heart of its
mortal dream' and join her and ride to that Faery realm of
forgetfulness and immortality to which she had seduced Oisin
(pronounced Usheen) in 'The Wanderings of Oisin', and which
Hanrahan also entered (in the *Stories of Red Hanrahan* and several
poems). The 'Sidhe' (pronounced 'shee' as in 'banshee', the

wailing ghost of Irish folktale) are the Faery folk who in Irish legend combine an idea of the souls of the dead with vague memories of the ancient inhabitants of the island, the Tuatha de Danaan, who left behind them long barrows and cromlechs. At certain times they ride abroad ('hosting') from the otherworld on wild horses, to abduct any mortals who cross their path. Yeats continues to use them as representatives of a menacing, alien, otherworldly order of things until his final poetry. Even in the early poem 'The Man who Dreamed of Faeryland', however, it is plain to see that for Yeats this is no fanciful sentimental realm for children to toy with. Rather the Sidhe are associated with that 'bitter black wind that blows from the left hand' and 'has bundled up the clouds high over Knocknarea' in 'Red Hanrahan's Song about Ireland'. Usually even Yeats's most fatuous 'faery' poetry has a dark edge.

The most famous instance of this 'Celtic Twilight' poetry is the much anthologised 'Lake Isle of Innisfree', with its vague desire for a peace that will come dropping slow from the eaves of the cabin he says he intends to build on his lake isle – perhaps one of the worst poems written by a great poet. But there are some achievements in the mode. 'Ephemera', for instance, adds vigour to its moods by turning them into a dialogue between lovers whose affair is at an end. The attitudinising is thus distanced as drama and narrative, taking place in a doom-laden landscape that puts their words in context. The ominous image of leaves falling 'like faint meteors in the gloom', and the man's final words, which offer an almost cynical consolation ('for other lovers await us;/Hate on and love through unrepining hours') make the '"continual farewell"' with which the poem ends less sentimental, presaging the mature Yeats's ability to weld conflicting emotions into a single sentence.

Yeats wrote to AE in 1904 of his desire to break with such 'exaggeration of sentiment & sentimental beauty which I have come to think unmanly'. His early popularity had arisen in part, he thought, from admiration for what he now saw as a 'weakness' exemplified by his play *The Land of Heart's Desire*. Although he had been 'fighting the prevalent decadence for years', he had only now conquered the 'sentiment & sentimental sadness, a womanish introspection'. He now believed that 'this region is full of false images of the spirit & of the body'. In fact,

'We possess nothing but the will & we must never let the children of vague desires breathe upon it nor the waters of sentiment rust the terrible mirror of its blade.' He went on to enunciate his new commitment to 'emotions . . . in which there is . . . an athletic joy'. In a letter to his friend Katharine Tynan as early as March 1888 Yeats had expressed his dissatisfaction with this kind of writing, citing as an instance the chorus to 'The Stolen Child':

> I have noticed . . . that it is almost all a flight into fairyland from the real world, and a summons to that flight . . . that it is not the poetry of insight and knowledge, but of longing and complaint – the cry of the heart against necessity. I hope some day to alter that and write poetry of insight and knowledge.

It was not, however, till the up-and-coming young American poet Ezra Pound impudently began to instruct the older poet in how to write, that Yeats came to realise this new style. It was to turn a minor versifier into a great poet. But before this, his experiences with the related realms of Irish politics and the Irish theatre had prepared him for the change.

2.4   MAUD GONNE AND THEATRE BUSINESS

'I was twenty-three years old when the troubling of my life began', Yeats wrote in his posthumously published *Memoirs* (p. 40). On 1 February 1889 he wrote from London to his friend, the nationalist leader John O'Leary:

> Miss Gonne came to see us the day before yesterday. I dined with her & her sister & cousin last night. She is not only very handsome but very clever. Though her politics in European matters be a little sensational. . . . It was pleasant however to hear her attacking a young military man from India who was there, on English rule in India. She is very Irish. . . . It was you, was it not, who converted Miss Gonne to her Irish opinions. She herself will make many converts.

The prediction was to prove correct, as was that of Yeats's sister Elizabeth, who wrote in her diary on 30 January: 'Miss Gonne, the Dublin beauty (who is marching on to glory over the hearts of the Dublin youths), called today on Willie. . . . She is immensely tall and very stylish and well dressed in a careless way. . . . She has a rich complexion and hazel eyes and is, I think, decidedly handsome. . . .' One of the hearts was Yeats's own. Though he was already, in sympathies at least, a nationalist, it was 'that straight back and arrogant head', remembered at the end of his life in 'Beautiful Lofty Things', which set the seal on his conversion.

Yeats's meeting with Maud Gonne in 1889 was to be crucial in shaping the rest of his life. Almost at once he fell in love with her. But that love was from the start mediated by a third element: Ireland. It was John O'Leary who had provided the fateful introduction, thus intervening for a second time in Yeats's life. For it was O'Leary too who, meeting Yeats for the first time in 1885, shortly after returning from twenty years of prison and exile, had first introduced the young poet to the idea of an Irish national literature, and set him reading Ferguson, Mangan and the Young Ireland poets of the 1840s, as he was to encourage his adaptations of tales from the ancient Irish epics translated by Standish O'Grady, Douglas Hyde (the first president of the Gaelic League), and Lady Gregory.

Here was a major challenge ready-made for a young and ambitious poet, one which fired Yeats at once: to 'know [Ireland] to the heart in all her moods', as he was to write to AE in 1898, and thus to become 'the poet of a people, the poet of a new insurrection'. And to do this for a beautiful young woman who seemed to personify Ireland. If Yeats induced Maud Gonne to join the Golden Dawn and his other spiritualist enterprises, she in turn led him deeper into the complicated factional politics of the Irish Republican Brotherhood. There was in fact a considerable overlap of members and ideas between the two networks, as well as the kind of correspondence in structure often shared by semi-clandestine sects of this kind in religion and politics. For both individuals, the idea of a spiritual otherworld represented by a strange amalgam of Irish myth, astrology, Judaeo-Christian heresies and Neo-Platonism, in which druid, priest and seer merged, was the other side of that political coin which placed a reborn Ireland as the antithesis to everything English, materialistic and base. She was to recall this phase in her essay on 'Yeats and Ireland' in *Scattering Branches: Tributes to the Memory of W. B. Yeats* (ed. Stephen Gwynn, 1940):

> The land of Ireland, we both felt, was powerfully alive and invisibly peopled, and whenever we grew despondent over the weakness of the nationalist movement, we went to it for comfort. If only we could make contact with the hidden forces of the land it would give us strength for the freeing of Ireland. (pp. 22–3)

Yeats promised Maud a play in which she could star as a heroine of the new Irish movement. He first wrote in 1891 *The Countess Cathleen*, in which an aristocratic Anglo-Irish lady sells her soul to the devil to free her peasants from oppression, but she did not perform the role. In 1902 she finally appeared in *Cathleen ni Houlihan*, a play which took its theme from the United Irishmen's uprising in 1798. In it she plays a part symbolically identified with Ireland itself – the 'poor old woman' which is one of the epithets for Ireland in Gaelic.

Yeats's turn to drama was an inevitable one for someone who wanted to write for Ireland. But it brought more political and practical implications than he had expected. In 1891 his literary enthusiasms had been for the dreamy lyric, and in so far as he acknowledged a darker world it was filtered through the decadent imagery of his friends in the Rhymers' Club in London, Lionel Johnson and Ernest Dowson, who had begun to anglicise Baudelaire's seamy Parisian underworld by writing of a romanticised London where every whore was a femme fatale and every drop-out and drunk a mystic of the flesh.

Yeats's first plays still belong to an Irish fantasy world of fatal passions and impossible dreams. But a sharper experience was reforming his intellect. In 1891, rejected in a marriage proposal by Maud Gonne, he set out to prove his nationalist credentials to her by establishing first the Irish Literary Society of London and, the following year, the National Literary Society in Dublin, with O'Leary as its president. The aim of both organisations was to further the Irish political cause by reawakening its literature. The success of this venture led to a scheme to set up small branch lending libraries throughout Ireland, as centres for literary and political education. Maud Gonne toured the country on behalf of this aim. He was to admit in *Memoirs* (p. 59) that in such work 'there was much patriotism, and more desire for a fair woman'. In 1908 he was to suggest in 'Words' that had he not constantly been impelled to make his 'darling' understand 'What I have done, or what would do / In this blind bitter land' he 'might have thrown poor words away / And been content to live', giving up his career of writing.

The literary crusade was soon, however, beset by the usual turbulent infighting associated with sectarian politics. Yeats was not prepared to tolerate literary mediocrity just because it professed the right national sentiments, while his opponents wanted to make 'correct' political views the criterion of worth. Opposing the model of the Young Ireland movement, Yeats was characteristically accused of being, he wrote later, 'under English influence – the influence of English decadent poets perhaps'. He was not helped in all this by Maud Gonne's indifference to the dispute: she had directed her energies to the more important question of peasant evictions, before returning to Paris in 1893.

A visit to Paris in 1894 brought Yeats another rejected proposal of marriage, but also more positive developments, including his first direct exposure to an alternative literary tradition. Through Arthur Symons he met the French Symbolist poets Mallarmé and Paul Verlaine, and saw Villiers de l'Isle-Adam's influential play *Axël*. The following year this experience was strengthened by sharing rooms in London for some months with Arthur Symons, who was shortly to publish the vastly influential study of modern French poetry, *The Symbolist Movement in Literature*, a book which was to be a landmark in the development of the whole 'Modernist' movement in literature, of which Yeats was to become a leading figure.

In 1896 his largely theoretical ideas of love were enlarged and enlightened by a year-long affair with Olivia Shakespear, called 'Diana Vernon' in his *Memoirs*. In this year, too, he met Lady Augusta Gregory and in Paris, where he had gone to found an order of Celtic Mysteries (!), his fellow Anglo-Irishman, John Synge. With both these people his literary career was hereafter to be inextricably entangled. He had also joined the IRB, and

cast himself as the impartial mediator who could bring together
the various nationalist factions into a single movement. In
furthering this aim, as in his literary politickings, Yeats showed
an unexpected flair for diplomacy, lobbying and constructive
argument. This was to stand him in good stead when the
creation of an Irish national theatre with the aid of Lady Gregory
and Edward Martyn became his main preoccupation from 1898
onwards.

Henceforward, a great deal of Yeats's activity was to be
directed to this goal, both by writing and encouraging the
writing of plays with a national theme, and by working to
establish a permanent venue for such work. In 1902 he became
the president of the Irish National Dramatic Society and Maud
Gonne played the title role of *Cathleen ni Houlihan* in Dublin.

Several proposals of marriage by Yeats in the previous years,
and a 'spiritual marriage' agreed between them in 1898, did
not, however, prevent her in 1903 from marrying Major John
MacBride, who had fought against the British in the Boer War.
Yeats's plays had been performed by the Irish National Theatre
Company in London, and he himself had gone on his first
lecture tour of the United States. But this new celebrity was no
compensation for the bitterness he felt over what he saw as
Maud Gonne's betrayal. In 1904 he threw his energies into the
business of being first a producer–manager and then co-director
with Lady Gregory and Synge of the newly-formed Abbey
Theatre in Dublin, the product of ten years of campaigning.
1907 brought the angry recriminations of the 'Abbey Riots' on
the first performance of Synge's *The Playboy of the Western World.*

The riots were worked up by a nationalist audience angry at
what they saw as Synge's slander of the Irish peasantry as a
body of parricidal young men and promiscuous young women.
There was much indignation at the use of the word 'shift'
(petticoat). Yeats, not shy and retiring when his blood was up,
was ready to confront the mob not only in print and on the
public platform but in the theatre itself, telling them on one
occasion 'You have disgraced yourselves again'. Several of his
poems evince this new contempt, reinforced for Yeats by the
public's venal response (also a subject for poems during this
period) to Sir Hugh Lane's generous offer of his collection of
Impressionist paintings to the City of Dublin, providing it
constructed a gallery worthy of them.

Not only the technical demands of dramatic writing and production, but the practical politics of 'Theatre business, management of men', what he calls in 'The Fascination of What's Difficult' 'the day's war with every knave and dolt', gave Yeats a new and realistic outlook on life. The bitterness over Maud Gonne, the new emotional sophistication that came from moving into an ever wider world, all contributed to change Yeats's attitude to life. With it came a new vigour and directness in his language and a new, harsh contentiousness in his themes. Increasingly, his poetry has a dramatic, combative quality. In the brief poem 'A Coat' in 1912 he announced his new programme. His previous poetry, he says, had been a coat 'Covered with embroideries/Out of old mythologies'. But the style was taken over by fools, who claimed it as their own. Now he has decided on a new, more honest (but potentially more dangerous) tack:

> Song, let them take it,
> For there's more enterprise
> In walking naked.

If Yeats in his later poetry comes perilously close to indecent exposure it was nevertheless this decision to walk naked that turned him into a major poet. All poetic 'enterprise' has an element of risk. For Yeats, the time was propitious, for English literature was about to see its rejuvenation at the hands of two émigré Americans, T. S. Eliot and Ezra Pound, and another Irishman, James Joyce. From being a perpetual 'enfant terrible' Yeats was to become the elder statesman of this new, literary insurrection. In 1908 he met for the first time Ezra Pound, newly arrived in Europe, by whom Yeats would soon be 'changed utterly', set to school to perfect his own potential greatness. In 1909 Yeats wrote what was at once an epitaph on the style of his youth (in life and art) and a manifesto for the great years to come, significantly linking life and art in a common project, 'The Coming of Wisdom with Time':

> Though leaves are many, the root is one;
> Through all the lying days of my youth

I swayed my leaves and flowers in the sun;
Now I may wither into the truth.

Yeats was 45. His real poetic life had only just begun. Seven years later, in 1917, after one last proposal to her and a desperate proposal to her natural daughter Iseult, he finally turned his back on the Maud Gonne delusion by marrying Georgie Hyde-Lees, by whom he had a daughter in 1919 and a son in 1921. In 1917 too he bought and began to renovate the Norman Tower at Ballylee which was to become the most potent symbol of his later poetry. He lived there only in the summer, buying other houses in Dublin and London. Walking naked in poetry involved, it seemed, the collection of a large amount of baggage and commitments in the historical world.

2.5   INDEPENDENCE STRUGGLE AND CIVIL WAR

In 'September 1913' Yeats expressed his disenchantment with the nationalist movement, dominated, as he saw it, by the values of the Catholic middle classes, believing that 'men were born to pray and save' and 'add the halfpence to the pence / And prayer to shivering prayer'. The poem's refrain is adamant about what has been lost: 'Romantic Ireland's dead and gone, / It's with O'Leary in the grave'. The events of the next few years were to show how ill-founded was such an assumption.

When war was declared between Germany and the British Empire in 1914, the majority of Irish citizens, Catholic as well as Protestant, were still opposed to complete Home Rule. What brought about the change in attitudes was the treatment by heavy-handed British authorities of the leaders of the Easter Rebellion, which broke out on 24 April 1916. R. M. Kain writes that, at the outbreak of war:

Members of the nationalist organisations had been ridiculed as ineffective, or despised as slackers. No military draft had been imposed on Ireland, but thousands volunteered. . . . It was fact that, after the surrender of the Post Office at the end of Easter Week, Irish prisoners were hissed by the crowds who watched them being led off to prison. Then came the

slow toll of executions, and the terrible beauty was born.
(D. E. S. Maxwell and S. B. Bushrui (eds), *W. B. Yeats 1865–1965. Centenary Essays*, p. 59)

The phrase 'terrible beauty' is from the poem 'Easter 1916', which records some of the perplexity of moderate, 'constitutional' nationalists like Yeats himself. The uprising was planned to take advantage of Britain's weakness, opening a second front behind the lines, in the expectation that a British defeat in the Great War would bring independence, on Wolfe Tone's principle that 'England's difficulty is Ireland's opportunity'. In this the republicans had been given military and logistical assistance by the German High Command.

About 700 republicans had begun the Rebellion by seizing strategic points in Dublin. Foremost of these was the Dublin Post Office, where Padraic Pearse and a squad of nationalist soldiers held on amidst heavy gunfire for several days, before being taken prisoner. Some died on the spot; others were executed for treason later. This event rapidly entered the national mythology, becoming part of the 'phantasmagoria', the collective dream of the new Irish state – in effect its foundation myth. At the end of his life, Yeats returned to the same scene for the authentic image of Irish nationhood, Pearse calling up Cuchulain, in 'The Statues'. But if Ireland was changed utterly by 'What stalked through the Post Office' in 1916, Yeats's poem was itself one factor in the transformation, turning defeat into victory and a squalid history into heroic national myth.

Another executed ringleader of the Rebellion mentioned in 'Easter 1916' was the trade union organiser and socialist, James Connolly, who, though reluctant to engage in armed struggle rather than the longer and more wide-reaching work of political and trade union agitation, had joined in out of loyalty. He figures also in 'The Rose Tree' and 'The O'Rahilly'. This late and powerfully melodramatic ballad records that The O'Rahilly too had fought to call off the Uprising, and persuaded his own Kerry men not to take part in what he regarded as a suicidal 'crazy fight'. But he then turned up at the Post Office himself to fight and die, saying, according to the poem, 'Because I helped to wind the clock / I come to hear it strike'.

'Easter 1916', published for the first time in a limited edition of 25 in September of that year and a highly seditious poem for wartime, is a declaration that Yeats accepts responsibility for his part in winding up the clock. When the poem reached a wider readership in 1920 it was in an issue of the socialist journal *The New Statesman* which contained several articles condemning the 'official terrorism' of the British forces in Ireland. Yeats was thus unequivocally identifying himself with the nationalist cause, even though, in the poem, he still speculates that even now 'England may keep faith' and implement the Home Rule promised in an Act of Parliament in 1914 but deferred by the outbreak of war.

It may be, he says, that 'excess of love / Bewildered' the rebels, leading them to foolhardy and unnecessary adventurism. It may be that their hearts have been 'Enchanted to a stone' by their obsessive, inhuman commitment to a single idea. But by now, such reservations are no longer relevant. The stone troubles the living stream, it is 'in the midst of all', and it can never now be ignored, for this insurrectionary act has transformed the whole political and moral landscape in which they live. The grey mediocre world of Dublin, where he once exchanged 'polite meaningless words' and 'a mocking tale or a gibe', a world of 'casual comedy' where motley (the jester's multicoloured patchwork) was worn, has been 'changed, changed utterly' by this act. The act of insurrection has *created* meaning in the midst of meaninglessness, forged a phantasmagoria which does not allow for fence-sitting or backsliding, but demands that people define themselves unequivocally for or against the Rebellion and its consequences.

Both actors and audience in this tragic drama have thus been changed. The once sweet voice of Constance Markiewicz, made shrill Yeats says by nights of political argument, is now transformed anew, into the thrilling tones of the tragic actress. Yeats too has been changed, sweeping aside his hesitations, now able to recognise the heroism even of John MacBride, Maud Gonne's estranged husband, whom he had merely it seems '*dreamed* / A drunken vainglorious lout'. Yet there is a sense in which Yeats is only briefly an extremist, the hint that this magical act of revolt has 'bewildered' him too out of his normal discriminations, enchanting him with illusory images of grandeur.

'Nineteen Hundred and Nineteen' is a poem about the last

stages of that revolt against British rule. In February of that year Yeats's daughter Anne had been born in Dublin. Some time between then and June of the same year he had written 'A Prayer for my Daughter', with its anxiety for her future, in an Ireland racked by violence, scarcely concealed in the image of a 'haystack- and roof-levelling wind', howling in from the sea with hardly an obstacle to block its force, as she sleeps on in her cradle. The 'great gloom' in the poet's mind is modified, however, by a certain almost euphoric agitation, as, 'in excited reverie', he imagines the future 'Dancing to a frenzied drum, / Out of the murderous innocence of the sea'. The *oxymoron* of 'murderous innocence' (adjective and noun as if in paradoxical contradiction) indicates just how ambiguous are his feelings here. Though he wishes later for 'radical innocence' and the 'custom and . . . ceremony' in which 'innocence and beauty [are] born', he cannot completely conceal that he is drawn to the violence and extremity, the 'Assault and battery' of that wind.

Yeats spent the summer of 1919 at Ballylee. During this period, the Irish Republican Army had begun a guerrilla war against British occupation, burning down the great houses of the Ascendancy as they went. The British government replied with a campaign of unsurpassed brutality against the civilian population, mainly carried out by units of Auxiliaries and what, from the colour of their uniforms, came to be known as the 'Black and Tans', special military units in some ways forerunners of the SAS. At the centre of 'Nineteen Hundred and Nineteen' is an anecdote which expresses the brutality of this war – an account of what the Black and Tans did in Gort, on Lady Gregory's demesne. Three years later he was to write to the English scholar Herbert Grierson of the current situation in Ireland:

I think things are coming right slowly, though very slowly; we have had years now of murder and arson in which both nations have shared impartially. In my own neighbourhood the Blacks and Tans dragged young men tied alive to a lorry by their heels till their bodies were rent in pieces. 'There was nothing for the mother but the head' said a country man, and the head he spoke of was found on the road side. The one enlivening truth that starts out of it all is that we may learn charity after mutual contempt. There is no longer a virtuous nation and the best of us live by candle light. (*Letters*, p. 690)

In 'Nineteen Hundred and Nineteen' Yeats could show none of this forbearance and attempt at impartiality. Indeed impartiality is there called into question as the delusion of a pre-war era that did not understand the real nature of the violence on which supposedly civilised society is founded. His contemporaries once had faith in 'A law indifferent to blame or praise, / To bribe or threat'. The word 'indifferent' slyly implies the actual contemptuous disregard for humane values underneath such attitudes, far removed from real impartiality. They assumed that progress was in the nature of things, that change would come inevitably from the steady and rational spreading of an argument: 'Public opinion ripening for so long / We thought it would outlive all future days'. Such beliefs were mere naïvety, and the revelation has been shattering. Their 'fine thought' was mere self-delusion. The 'worst rogues and rascals' had not died out but were simply biding their time, and have now returned with renewed viciousness:

> Now days are dragon-ridden, the nightmare
> Rides upon sleep; a drunken soldiery
> Can leave the mother, murdered at her door,
> To crawl in her own blood, and go scot-free;
> The night can sweat with terror as before
> We pieced our thoughts into philosophy,
> And planned to bring the world under a rule,
> Who are but weasels fighting in a hole.

In December 1921 the Anglo-Irish Treaty was signed. By this, the British government agreed to cede independence as a Dominion within the Commonwealth to the 'Irish Free State' in exchange for a cessation of hostilities. As a result of Lloyd George's Amending Act of 1920, however, six of the nine counties of Ulster in the north, where there was a Protestant majority, were to remain under the British Crown, with their own devolved parliament, Stormont, in Belfast.

Almost at once, civil war broke out in the south between

those nationalists prepared to accept this compromise (led by the new President Arthur Griffith and the former military leader of the nationalist forces, Michael Collins) and the irredentists under Eamon de Valera, who would not accept the oath of allegiance, arguing instead for the reunification of Ireland outside the Commonwealth. These elements constituted themselves as the authentic Irish Republican Army and conducted a guerrilla war against the 'turncoats' of the new Irish parliament, or Dail. In 1922 they assassinated Collins in an ambush. Civil war raged until 1923, when de Valera ordered a ceasefire, though it was to be nine years before he came to power with the election of a Fianna Fail government which rescinded the Anglo-Irish Treaty.

Yeats, by this time once more disenchanted with politics, placed his sympathies with the 'moderates' in the government, and early in 1922, in the same month that his father died in New York, accepted nomination to be a senator in the upper house of the Dail, something which brought him death threats from the IRA. (In 1915 he had refused a knighthood from the British Crown, though he had a few years earlier accepted a Civil List pension from the same source.) The violent birthpangs of the new state produced the despair, anguish and anger of 'Meditations in Time of Civil War'.

Near the end of his life Yeats fretted in 'The Man and the Echo' over his own responsibility for this violence, asking, perhaps with an element of self-importance, of his nationalist play *Cathleen ni Houlihan*:

> Did that play of mine send out
> Certain men the English shot?
> . . . Could my spoken words have checked
> That whereby a house lay wrecked?

He had already, however, accepted responsibility in 'Meditations', seeing the casual assassinations, skirmishes, and the burning of the ancestral houses by IRA Irregulars as signs of that mere anarchy which had been loosed upon the world. Because 'we had fed the heart on fantasies, / The heart's grown brutal from the fare; / More substance in our enmities / Than in our love . . .' All that is left is the empty house of the stare (starling), and even the honey-bees and the mother birds bringing grubs to their young, symbols of vitality and nurture, are building in the loosening wall of a threatened house. The house itself is visited by soldiers of both sides, yet these are not monsters but ordinary men, the IRA Irregular 'affable', 'heavily built' like Falstaff, 'cracking jokes of civil war', the government Lieutenant patiently listening to Yeats's complaints about the weather, and the poet secretly envying each in turn his casualness and competence. The readiness to accept the 'We' of a collective guilt (and punishment) binds the poem together as its discrete scraps of information pull it apart. In a powerful dramatic presentation of the disintegration it describes, Yeats's syntax in this fifth section falls apart into isolated clauses and phrases, unable to make coherent sense of the anarchy it vividly depicts:

> We are closed in, and the key is turned
> On our uncertainty; somewhere
> A man is killed, or a house burned,
> Yet no clear fact to be discerned:
> Come build in the empty house of the stare.
>
> A barricade of stone or of wood;
> Some fourteen days of civil war;
> Last night they trundled down the road
> That dead young soldier in his blood. . . .

The sequence closes with a poem whose very title indicates the despair into which the poet has sunk, in a world which seems drowned in mindless violence and vendetta and 'the embrace of nothing': 'I see Phantoms of Hatred and of the Heart's Fullness and of the Coming Emptiness'. In such a future, 'A mist that is like blown snow is sweeping over all', reducing all distinction and excellence to 'senseless tumult', the 'complacency' of a world that takes violence for granted, and the 'brazen hawks' of 'an indifferent multitude', the rule of the mob. It is out of this brutal disenchantment, this anger and contempt for a democracy collapsing into 'mere anarchy' that the mood of Yeats's later poetry is to emerge.

2.6 MATURITY AND OLD AGE

Yeats's emergent greatness, reaching its maturity in *The Wild Swans at Coole* and *Michael Robartes and the Dancer*, was given international recognition with the award of the Nobel Prize for Literature in 1923. By some commentators the last volume was seen as a kind of natural plateau, beyond which Yeats was not expected to progress. Few expected the new and passionate intensity that was to come in the last two decades of his life, with the production of four major volumes of poetry which turned from melancholy at lost love and anger at Ireland's plight to the raging against old age of *The Tower* (1928), the mellowed indignation in which dead and dying friends and the passing of Ascendancy greatness are evoked, and linked, in *The Winding Stair* (1933), and the renewed frenzy of *A Full Moon in March* (1935).

In the posthumously published *Last Poems* of 1939 he returned to all his old themes with a new fury of recall, balancing them all, bringing all to mind, setting the seal on old loves and passions, having the last word on his past and that of Ireland, and calling into question the value and importance of all he had done. The mood of this period is best indicated by two poems which stand almost in antithesis in this volume. 'What Then?' challenges every achievement of his life, literary success, money, friends, family, a home, an admiring circle, with the repeated cynical question in the refrain, '"What then?" sang Plato's ghost, "what then?"' Even his final stand against the dissolution of meaning, insisting that he 'Something to perfection brought', is capped by the questioning of this ironically ghostly spokesman of the eternal and abiding. 'The Municipal Gallery Revisited' finds in 'the images of thirty years' collected in the gallery much to think on about the transitory in human affairs, with its portraits of dead friends and acquaintances and scenes from the independence struggle. The poem finds Yeats for a time 'in despair that time may bring / Approved patterns of women or of men / But not the self-same excellence again.' The platonic ideal forms ('patterns') may repeat themselves, he says, but the unique individuals who embodied them are gone forever. Yet by the end of the poem he has reached a different mood, calling on those who come after to judge him not by his books alone but by the portraits of his friends gathered here. These are not merely personal acquaintances, but rather figures transformed into heroic symbols by history and art alike, actors on the stage of history for whom the next generation will be an audience, thus enabling them to outlive their passing:

> Ireland's history in their lineaments trace;
> Think where man's glory most begins and ends,
> And say my glory was I had such friends.

In his last years, Yeats is much aware of his public standing, the 'sixty-year-old smiling public man' of 'Among School Children'. He is the senator concerned with educational policy, in charge of the committee responsible for Ireland's new coinage, who speaks out on behalf of the Protestant minority in the divorce debate in the Dail in 1925. Internationally acclaimed, everywhere he travels he carries Ireland's reputation with him. Yet this does not lead him to a style of acceptance and decline into a genteel old age. Instead, his poetry is charged with a new and ferocious vigour. As he says in 'The Spur', it is spurred into song by 'lust and rage' which 'dance attendance upon my old age'. Not only on the personal front does this obtain. In politics too Yeats refuses to lapse into senescent calm. On the contrary, if anything he becomes more extremist and opinionated than in his youth, espousing for a while in the 1930s the cause of Irish Fascism. Even election in 1937 to the Athenaeum Club in London, the place where the British upper classes exchange their mocking tales and gibes, does not prevent him from publishing the following year 'The Ghost of Roger Casement', with its railing against the 'roar of mockery' and the beanfeasts and banquets of John Bull's Empire.

Discussing in April 1934 the indifference and even hostility in Ireland towards culture in general and the Abbey Theatre in particular, Yeats wrote of visiting members of Cosgrave's or de Valera's governments to protest about some attack or other on the arts:

> and upon each occasion I came away with the conviction that the Minister felt exactly as I felt but was helpless: the mob reigned. If that reign is not broken our public life will move

from violence to violence, or from violence to apathy; our Parliament disgrace and debauch those that enter it; our men of letters live like outlaws in their own country. It will be broken when some government seeks unity of culture not less than economic unity.

In the theatre, he says, quoting Victor Hugo, '"the mob becomes a people"', finding an image of itself which it can live up to. But Yeats then turns his analogy inside-out. History itself is 'some great theatre', in which a nation should be at once actors and audience, 'watching the sacred drama of its own history'. To act its part well that nation must have the unity of culture which comes from true self-knowledge. This knowledge is not acquired 'through abstractions, statistics, time tables, through images that refuse to compose themselves into a clear design. Such knowledge thins the blood. To know it in the concrete we must know it near at hand.'

It is here that Yeats's philosophy and vision of art link with his idea of nationality. The emphasis on lived, concrete 'blood' knowledge, as opposed to the abstractions of the intellect, is part of the Fascist philosophy, and it was indeed to such a politics that Yeats began to look for Ireland's salvation. A unified sensibility, he says, can be brought about only by instituting a different kind of social order:

> If any Government or party undertake this work it will need force, marching men . . . it will promise not this or that measure but a discipline, a way of life.

But, says Yeats, speaking of his 'Three Marching Songs', 'There is no such government or party today; should either appear I offer it these trivial songs and what remains to me of life'. This is false naïvety, and in August of the same year he added an even more ingenuous postscript, as if by way of apology:

> P.S. Because a friend belonging to a political party wherewith I had once some loose associations, told me that it had, or was about to have, or might be persuaded to have, some such aim as mine, I wrote these songs. Finding that it neither

would nor could, I increased their fantasy, their extravagance, their obscurity, that no party might sing them.

The party was in fact the 'Blueshirts', or Irish Fascists, led by General Eoin O'Duffy, who later led a brigade to fight in the Spanish Civil War on the side of the Fascist General Franco. Yeats's songs are clear in their sentiments. They proclaim that '"a good strong cause and blows are delight"', and urge us to hammer down fanatic and clown and drown all the dogs. And they offer to 'nations . . . empty up there at the top,/When order has weakened or faction is strong', the Fascist solution of marching men. Yeats certainly knew what he (and O'Duffy) were about, for he wrote to Olivia Shakespear in July 1933 (just after Hitler had come to power in Germany):

> The great secret is now out, – a convention of Blueshirts – 'National Guards' – have received their new leader with the Fascist salute, and the new leader announces reform of Parliament as his business. When I wrote to you the Fascist organiser of the Blueshirts had told me that he was about to bring to see me the man he had selected for leader that I might talk my anti-democratic philosophy. I was ready, for I had just rewritten for the seventh time the part of *A Vision* that deals with the future.

Yeats does go on to say of the new order he envisages: 'Doubtless I shall hate it (though not so much as I hate Irish democracy)'. But this is not to disown it. It is a melodramatic steeling of himself to accept what he saw as the unpalatable but necessary rigour of Fascism. His argument romanticises this with a clichéd metaphor which implies a link between his own old age and the decline and fall of his civilisation: 'but it is September, and we must not behave like the gay young sparks of May and June. Swinburne calls September "the month of the long decline of roses".'

There is something distasteful in the idea of this old man, close to death, taking a self-satisfied delight in his own toughness at the prospect of a coming holocaust. Certainly, we do no justice to the greatness of Yeats's poetry if, like critics such as Ellmann (*The Man and the Masks*, pp. 280–3) and his biographer

Joseph Hone (*W. B. Yeats: 1865–1939*, pp. 438–40) we try to downplay his authoritarian and anti-democratic views. It is much better to face up to them, as in the classic essays by George Orwell (see Chapter 1) and Conor Cruise O'Brien. The line of apologia taken by W. H. Auden (see Chapter 1) is developed with extensive documentation and illuminating readings of the work in Elizabeth Cullingford's *Yeats, Ireland and Fascism*. In the end, however, the special pleading is as conspicuous as in Orwell's and O'Brien's essays (see the final section of the Guide to Further Reading).

The fear of degeneration and decline, as in 'A Bronze Head' or 'The Statues', is what moves Yeats to this intemperate and at times fanatical fury against what the first song calls 'Those fanatics [who] all that we would do undo'. These fanatics for Yeats are also clowns. In Yeats's eyes they belong to that unmannerly and democratic rabble who represent the new ill-breeding in Ireland, and their plebeian fanaticism is therefore to be distinguished from his own aristocratic fanaticism, celebrated as part of his authentic Irish inheritance at the very moment that it is apologised for in a poem such as 'Remorse for Intemperate Speech'.

Throughout his work Yeats employs the language of theatre to express his vision of history (see, for example, the concise version of this in 'Two Songs from a Play'). In the prefatory note to 'Three Songs' Yeats wrote that he had come to fear 'that our growing disorder, the fanaticism that inflamed it like some old bullet imbedded in the flesh, was about to turn our noble history into an ignoble farce'. The martyrs of 'Easter 1916' had turned a 'casual comedy' into a heroic tragedy worthy of Parnell. 'We begin to live when we have conceived life as tragedy', Yeats wrote in 'The Trembling of the Veil'. Now he feared that Ireland would turn its back on such 'heroic reverie', and sink once again into the farce of knaves and clowns. The knaves and clowns were all of the left. The disorder he feared was not that of Fascism but of Communism, or 'Bolshevism'. The fear was to haunt his later years. Fascism, he believed, would restore 'the rule of the able and educated, man's old delight in submission'. That O'Duffy was a buffoon unworthy of Yeats's admiration, and his Fascist attitudinising a familiar kind of Ruritanian knockabout, does not seem to have struck the ageing poet.

Yeats's later years are characterised by a bitterness and fury that arises from his sense of a series of lost opportunities not so much for himself as for Ireland. He rages against age and 'bodily decrepitude', certainly, but his personal life seems increasingly satisfactory. A devoted wife and passionate encounters with younger women seem to have left him merely discontented with a decline in physical performance overcome for a while by the Steinach operation he had in 1934.

In 'Blood and the Moon' he had identified with 'Swift beating on his breast in sybilline frenzy blind / Because the heart in his blood-sodden breast had dragged him down into mankind'. A large part of what, following Swift, he thought of as his '*Saeva Indignatio*', or 'savage indignation', can be attributed to a similar love–hate for the impossible island to which he had linked his destiny. Life Swift, he had a sense that Ireland had failed him, failed to be that heroic, mythic country he had envisaged in his writings, remaining, instead, the homeland of Paudeen and Biddy, a dull, prosaic, narrow-minded, priest-ridden provincial backwater, not the 'Ireland poets have imagined, terrible and gay' of 'The Municipal Gallery Revisited'. The espousal of Fascism, like the apocalyptic vision of history in *A Vision*, first published in 1925, seem to issue from this larger dissatisfaction.

In his last poems, we find him constantly oscillating between raging against death and reclaiming everything in the undying images of art. Yeats himself was never sure where his loyalties finally lay – with the passing ephemeral moment or with the art which preserves it for a while but also ultimately goes down in the fire. Nothing survives of the Greek sculptor Callimachus' acclaimed handiwork in bronze or marble, he wrote in 'Lapis Lazuli'. In the perspective of eternity, empires and their art alike stand but a day. Yet, in the end, though all things fall and are built again, it is the gaiety of the artist and of the art that 'transfigur[es] all that dread'.

In *Autobiographies* Yeats wrote, in retrospect of his life:

If I found myself a director of men's consciences, or becoming any kind of idealized figure in their minds, I would, or I fancy I would, display or even exaggerate my frailties. All creation is from conflict, whether with our own mind or with that of others, and the historian who dreams of bloodless victory wrongs the wounded veterans. (p. 576)

A wounded veteran of Irish history himself, Yeats died in France on 28 January 1939, seven months before a new world war broke out in Europe. Almost ten years later, the war over, he was reinterred in Drumcliff Churchyard, Co. Sligo, under Ben Bulben mountain, among the bones of his Anglo-Irish ancestors. Theatrical to the last, he instructed that his gravestone be carved with the closing lines of the poem 'Under Ben Bulben', which is usually published at the end, as a kind of last will and testament, of any volume of his poems:

> Cast a cold eye
> On life, on death.
> Horseman, pass by!

But this injunction to the future, as if even in death he must have the last word, is too final, and too coldly austere, to be the measure of the real Yeats. Always a dialectical writer, convinced that 'all creation is from conflict' (*Autobiographies*, p. 576) and, with Blake, that 'without contraries is no progression', he would be better fitted with an epitaph which catches the perpetual incompleteness of things, the oscillation between extremes out of which he had constructed some of his finest poetry. The brief poem 'The Choice' might serve as an alternative epitaph. Equally theatrical but more dramatic, its last, balancing antithesis is not a conclusion but the prelude to something else. It points to a resolution which lies always in the poem's future as long as there are new generations to read, as if for the first time, 'all that story', and thus redeem vanity and remorse in the perpetual reclamation of art:

> The intellect of man is forced to choose
> Perfection of the life, or of the work,
> And if it take the second must refuse
> A heavenly mansion, raging in the dark.
> When all that story's finished, what's the news?
> In luck or out the toil has left its mark:

That old perplexity an empty purse,
Or the day's vanity, the night's remorse.

3
Yeats's Themes and Motifs

3.1 HOW THEMES ARE EMBODIED IN A POEM

The *theme* of a poem is its dominant idea, its *subject-matter* perceived as a concept. The subject-matter of 'The Wild Swans at Coole', for example, may be a landscape and the creatures, including the swans, which inhabit it, and the poet's feelings about it. But the theme could be said to be the idea of change and mutability. Very often we speak loosely of a theme when a more appropriate word would be *motif*, a recurrent image or idea. In the following, I have organised Yeats's themes around a variety of key concepts and images, 'motifs' in this sense. Analysing a poet's themes is complicated by the fact that such themes are usually not presented directly, but are present *implicitly* in a poem. They are, that is, *embodied* in the poem, and have to be read out or deduced by us, from a particular description of events or place, the evocation of a mood or feeling, an image or cluster of images. What the poet declares to be the theme of the poem, by fixing a particular title to it, may mislead us, and then part of the meaning of the poem is this very discrepancy between its declared and its actual theme. The latter is sometimes called a *subtext*.

A poem is likely to have more than one theme, particularly when, like 'The Tower' or 'Nineteen Hundred and Nineteen', it is a long poem with several sections and many shifts of mood and reference. Sometimes these themes jostle each other for attention, creating a kind of dramatic tension between the different impulses a poem contains. This *dramatic interplay* of themes is particularly important in Yeats's poetry. We may, as in 'The Tower', begin by feeling that the theme is anger at age and decline, and then find that the poet is talking about lost and unrequited love. But before we have assimilated this we see that he is affirming the pride of the Anglo-Irish tradition, and linking this to his own poetic achievements. A poem of any

55

There are many interlocking themes expressed/explored by Yeats in the poem...

complexity will articulate several, often interlocking themes.

Much of the lyric poet's skill in embodying his themes lies in the creation of what Yeats in 'The Circus Animals' Desertion' called 'masterful images'. The image, or symbol, is not something that can easily be made to give a clear and unequivocal meaning. When Yeats, for example, uses the image of the moon in his poems, it does not always mean ('stand for') the same thing. Sometimes it is literally just the moon, the source of a certain kind of light. But because its light is less revealing than the sun's, it can be associated with the mysterious workings of the poetic imagination, which is opposed in 'The Tower' to 'the prosaic light of day'.

In the poem which sets forth his doctrine of history, 'The Phases of the Moon', each of the twenty-eight nights of the waxing and waning moon are associated, somewhat arbitrarily, with certain types of personality and periods of history. At other times, more generally, it simply matters whether the moon is waxing or waning in a poem to indicate whether it is concerned with themes of aspiration or decline. The moon, like many of Yeats's images, is such a traditional symbol that it carries many accumulated associations with it, and these will call up many different themes. Poets have traditionally linked it, for example, with the kind of aloof, disdainful and mysterious beauty in women which Yeats finds in Maud Gonne. At the same time, its ancient associations with madness ('lunacy') can either reinforce or work against such an association. In 'The Tower' 'the brightness of the moon' is associated with wits driven astray by 'a peasant girl commended by a song'. But neither of these associations can explain a line like 'Banished heroic mother moon and vanished' in 'Lines Written in Dejection'.

In his essay 'The Symbolism of Poetry' Yeats discusses a passage from Burns's poetry in which the moon takes on just such a mysterious and unanalysable *polyvalency* – that is, it means many different things at the same time. Any one image, he suggests, if it is at all powerful, will probably have many associations, supplied by general culture or by the overall context of the poet's work.

In Yeats's poetry symbol and image are not only *devices* he uses to present his themes, but they are also themes in themselves. This will be discussed in the section on 'Symbol' below.

There is a further complication in Yeats's handling of his themes. Yeats is a highly *allusive* poet. That is, in calling up his themes, he frequently alludes to events and characters in myth and history or in the world around him with which the reader may not be acquainted. In his case, this includes not only the more familiar territory of classical, Greek and Roman culture, but also Irish legend and history, esoteric religion and philosophy (i.e. that which is known only to a few), and his own elaborate system of belief, particularly as set out in *A Vision*. Many of his friends and ancestors he refers to by name, assuming that we should know to whom he refers, though often our only knowledge of them is derived from his poems. Some of the key figures and events of his day are discussed in the biographical section.

Hugh Kenner, in an illuminating essay called 'The Sacred Book of the Arts' (see Guide to Further Reading, section 3), has argued that the best context in which to understand the allusions of a poem is that of the other poems in the same volume. The 'Ledaean body' of 'Among School Children', for example, can be explained by reference to the poem 'Leda and the Swan', which can be found on the preceding page of *The Tower*, and the images of its final stanza can be elucidated by reference to the poem 'Oedipus at Colonus', which comes on the following page. Nevertheless, at some point, it may be necessary to look up a dictionary of classical or Irish mythology, or a history of the modern world, to see the full significance of an allusion.

To sum up, there is no fixed theme that we can assume any one poem is 'about'. If there were, there would be no scope for the wide range of sometimes quite contradictory interpretations Yeats's poetry has attracted. But this should not be a discouragement but rather an encouragement. Yeats said that 'man can embody truth but he cannot know it'. For him, image and symbol are ways in which truths are concretely embodied, in all their richness and complexity. There is not some 'meaning' behind the poem, waiting for us to tear away the veils of language to come upon its naked 'theme'. Rather the words themselves, the lived experience of the whole poem, in its shifting moods and images, *are* the meaning. The themes are only there when a reader finds them, and so long as a poet can have new readers there is the possibility of new readings – that is, of finding new themes.

In what follows, I have tried to help the reader by picking out a few of the recurring and most obvious themes, often embodied in a single image or images, or suggested by recurrent allusions, which readers have traditionally found in Yeats. This is intended simply as a set of signposts on the way to the reader's own direct encounter with the poems.

3.2 SYMBOL AND IMAGE

The idea of the symbol is central to understanding Yeats's poetry. The symbol to be successful has to be mysterious, indefinable. In the essay 'William Blake' Yeats distinguishes between symbol and *allegory*. In an allegory, the allegorical figure stands directly for something else. In, for example, *Pilgrim's Progress*, the 'Giant Despair' with whom Christian fights stands directly for the condition of despair with which the Christian soul has to struggle. The symbol, by contrast, cannot be pinned down to a simple meaning. Its power and magic derive from its indefinability. It is by being unanalysable that the symbol supposedly offers access to a deeper reality. The cross in Yeats's early poetry, like the rose, another traditional symbol, cannot be said to represent any one thing clearly and unmistakably.

For Yeats, the symbol has a 'visionary' dimension. It offers a 'revelation'. He assumes, following Blake, 'the indissoluble marriage of all great art with symbol':

> There have been allegorists and teachers of allegory in plenty, but the symbolic imagination, or as Blake preferred to call it, 'vision', is not allegory, being 'a representation of what actually exists really and unchangeably'. A symbol is indeed the only possible expression of some invisible essence, a transparent lamp about a spiritual flame; while allegory is one of many possible representations of an embodied thing, or familiar principle . . . the one is a revelation, the other an amusement. (C, p. 22)

In his essay 'The Symbolism of Poetry' Yeats speaks of the symbol's function as 'evocation' and 'suggestion' and cites (and misquotes) as an example of 'the continuous indefinable symbolism which is the substance of all style' two lines from a poem of Burns's: 'The white moon is setting behind the white wave, / And Time is setting with me, O!' He comments:

> Take from them the whiteness of the moon and of the wave, whose relation to the setting of Time is too subtle for the intellect, and you take from them all their beauty. But, when all together . . . they evoke an emotion which cannot be evoked by any other arrangement of colours and sounds and forms. (*C*, p. 45)

That Burns actually wrote of 'the wan moon' suggests that Yeats's theory lacks something of substance here, but it is typical of him that anything as simple as mere objective fact should not get in the way of his imagination. He goes on to speak of symbolism's magical power to 'evoke indefinable and yet precise emotions, or, as I prefer to think, call down among us certain disembodied powers, whose footsteps over our heart we call emotions'.

When he speaks of this as 'the god it calls among us' we can see that even political events like the Easter Rebellion, calling into being 'A terrible beauty', summoning Cuchulain to Pearse's side, share in the symbolic imagination. In 'The Second Coming' the 'vast image out of *Spiritus Mundi*' is such a symbol, called up out of the 'spirit of the world', what Yeats elsewhere speaks of as the 'great Memory or . . . some mysterious tide in the depth of our being' (*C*, p. 76).

Part of the power of the symbol is that it always carries a surplus of meaning. It is charged with a significance in excess of what, following scientific method, we can pin on it. This is what makes it visionary and magical, and it is this *polyvalency* which, for Yeats, guarantees that it rises up from the deepest recesses of the collective unconscious. Yeats wrote in 'The Philosophy of Shelley's Poetry':

> It is only by ancient symbols, by symbols that have numberless meanings besides the one or two the writer lays an emphasis upon, or the half-score he knows of, that any highly subjective

art can escape from the barrenness and shallowness of a too
conscious arrangement, into the abundance and depth of
Nature. The poet of essences and pure ideas must seek in the
half-lights that glimmer from symbol to symbol as if to the
ends of the earth, all that the epic and dramatic poet finds of
mystery and shadow in the accidental circumstances of life.
(C, p. 72)

This account is steeped in the language of the Celtic Twilight,
with its essences and pure ideas and glimmers and half-lights.
But there is nothing here which cannot be applied to the theory
of the image of the mature Yeats. At the end of the essay,
indeed, Yeats changes from the word 'symbol' to that of 'image',
thereby prefiguring his later writing. This word seems to have
a more precise meaning in poems such as 'Byzantium' or 'Among
School Children'. But on examination it takes on the same
indefinable and supernatural quality. 'Among School Children'
tells us that 'Both nuns and mothers worship images'. Although
these are the icons of Madonna and Christ-child to be found in
any Catholic church, they are also more intangible images –
visions in the mind of what is signified by the idea of mother
and child. Even the living baby upon the mother's lap can
become a symbol of something more, as the schoolgirl standing
before the poet becomes a living image of how Maud Gonne
looked when young.

In 'Shelley' (C, p. 79) this is spelt out in language which
explains some of the imagery of the later poems, such as the
self-consuming fire of 'Sailing to Byzantium' and 'Byzantium'.
Yeats speaks of

. . . how there is for every man some one scene, some one
adventure, some one picture that is the image of his secret
life, for wisdom first speaks in images, and that this one
image, if he would but brood over it his life long, would lead
his soul, disentangled from unmeaning circumstance and the
ebb and flow of the world, into that far household where the
undying gods await all whose souls have become simple as a
flame.

3.3   FALCON, DOVE, SWAN

We can see how Yeats's symbols work by considering some of his most frequent images – in this case, his bird imagery. His falcon in 'The Second Coming', for example, may 'stand for' a violence and cruel rapacity which has broken free of control, turning and turning in the widening gyres of history. But this bird of prey is a symbol too fraught with accumulated historical meanings to be so pinned down. It also represents the aristocratic and stately world associated with medieval falconry. In its wide-ranging flight it is also an image of grace and beauty and the free spirit.

The section of *A Vision* called 'Dove or Swan' links the divine rape of Leda by Zeus in the guise of a swan with the impregnation of the Virgin Mary by the Holy Ghost. The Holy Ghost descends in the form of a dove at the annunciation of another semi-divine transformer of history, Christ, so that, in the words of 'The Second Coming', 'twenty centuries of stony sleep / Were vexed to nightmare by a rocking cradle'. Dove and swan here initiate and 'stand for' antithetical moments of history.

But elsewhere the swan is endowed with other, often contradictory associations. Yeats sometimes seems to use it in a semi-allegorical way, as for example when he observes in 'Nineteen Hundred and Nineteen':

> Some moralist or mythological poet
> Compares the solitary soul to a swan.

But though he goes on to say 'I am satisfied with that,' in fact Yeats's own expansion takes it beyond a mere comparison. The swan as symbol takes off from being merely an allegorical emblem. Yeats's description of its flight calls our attention to the bird as 'a living thing', an 'image' fully realised in all its flesh and blood particularity. As a result, the 'soul' takes second place to the image which is supposed to figure it, and becomes as rich and mysterious in its significance as the bird itself. Soul and swan seem to fuse – an effect achieved by the ambiguity of the pronoun 'it', which could and in effect does refer to both, making each the mirror of the other:

Satisfied if a troubled mirror show it,
Before that brief gleam of its life be gone,
An image of its state;
The wings half spread for flight,
The breast thrust out in pride
Whether to play, or to ride
Those winds that clamour of approaching night.

The poet then turns to consider the soul in a formula that repeats the construction of the opening analogy ('Some Platonist affirms . . .') before coming back in the next stanza to the physical, embodied image of the swan. This return totally transforms the argument, cutting it short with a powerful and concrete natural rebuke to all this abstract speculation. The 'image', by taking on a life of its own, as a real creature out there in the wind and water, ceases to be merely an illustration of something else. It becomes in addition an element in the argument itself, which challenges the 'desolate heaven' of thought. It even threatens to cut short the act of writing the poem itself:

The swan has leaped into the desolate heaven:
That image can bring wildness, bring a rage
To end all things, to end
What my laborious life imagined, even
The half-imagined, the half-written page.

Even, then, when Yeats seems to be speaking 'allegorically', his symbolical imagination takes over, and turns *abstract* analogy into *living* correspondence.

There is a similar movement in the third section of 'The Tower'. Yeats's strong visual imagination transforms the cliché of the dying bird's 'swan song' into a powerful and emotive figure in an argument that proceeds not through logical abstractions but through a succession of concrete images. Or again, in 'Coole Park and Ballylee', Yeats seems to be writing of the swan simply as an 'emblem' of some spiritual abstraction (the soul). But the concrete precision with which the bird is described turns us away from the abstract correspondence to the real creature:

At sudden thunder of the mounting swan
I turned about and looked where branches break
The glittering reaches of the flooded lake.

Another emblem there! That stormy white
But seems a concentration of the sky;
And, like the soul, it sails into the sight
And in the morning's gone, no man knows why;
And is so lovely that it sets to right
What knowledge or its lack had set awry,
So arrogantly pure, a child might think
It can be murdered with a spot of ink.

What happens is that the soul is deployed to explain the swan, and not vice versa. The scene is described in such specific detail that its emblematic meaning is overwhelmed by the physical sights and sounds.

3.4 IMAGINATION AND REALITY

'Coole Park and Ballylee' is a poem rich in themes. It raises, for example, the whole question of how a once meaningful tradition, symbolised by the stately house at Coole Park, is now under threat. It raises too, in the image of the ageing Lady Gregory, the theme of age, and it calls up also, in its reference to 'The book of the people', the relation between the poet and the Irish people. But perhaps the most relevant theme to follow up here, since it arises from all these others, is Yeats's preoccupation with how the imagination not only interprets but transforms the real world.

In the passage quoted at the end of the last section, the mind plays a key role. It is human perception ('looked', 'seems', 'knows', 'think') which interprets the bird now as an intellectual emblem and now as a physical object, no more than 'a concentration of the sky'. (The pun on the word 'concentration' relates to both mental and physical aspects.)

For Yeats, the imagination is quite literally an *image-making power*. That is, it thinks in concrete realities, not abstractions. In 'The Tower' he indicates that his imagination will never be content to 'deal / In abstract things'; and he 'send[s] imagination forth' to call up 'Images and memories / From ruin or from ancient trees'. This is exactly what the imagination is doing in this poem, in seeking everywhere emblems of its spiritual state and preoccupations.

The child mistakes the real creature, the swan, for no more than a sign, a mark on paper. This whole poem toys with and repeatedly rejects the idea that the physical world is only a symbol of something beyond. The opening stanza, in all its concrete detail – window-ledge, waters, otters, moorhens, Raftery's cellar, the rocky place in Coole demesne, the lake and the hole – contradicts the abstract generalisation of its last line: 'What's water but the generated soul?'

When in the fourth and fifth stanzas Yeats turns to the human scene, the same interplay occurs between what people and places *are* and what they *symbolise* – between the sound of a stick on the floor and the old woman who wields it. The sound becomes a symbol not only of Lady Gregory but of age itself. Similarly, beloved books become symbols of the 'famous hands' that bound them, marbles, pictures, rooms become symbols of the 'travelled men and children' who once lived at Coole Park as well as of the genteel tradition they body forth. The 'last inheritor' of that tradition, Lady Gregory, bereaved of her only son, in turn becomes a figure symbolising, summing up, both that tradition and its demise.

3.5 HOUSE AND TOWER

What Yeats is suggesting here is that a whole tradition can be symbolised by its most impressive achievements. The imagination responds to and reads out that tradition from its monuments. In the present case, these monuments are the country houses of the Anglo-Irish Ascendancy, another of Yeats's recurrent themes.

'Coole Park, 1929' and 'Coole Park and Ballylee, 1931' focus Yeats's attitudes towards this ambiguous inheritance. The 'Ancestral Houses' celebrated in the first poem of 'Meditations' sum up this ambivalence. The poem tells us they were built by 'Some violent bitter man, some powerful man' who 'Called architect and artist in, that they, / Bitter and violent men, might rear in stone / The sweetness that all longed for night and day, / The gentleness none there had ever known.' They represent for him a culture and gentility emerging from but untainted by that world of violence. It may be in the end, however, that such monuments to graciousness simply 'take our greatness with our violence'. They are not really free from it.

The house is not necessarily a symbol of security. It can, for example, be the Gothic mansion inhabited by dark forces. In Yeats's poetry the house is a complex symbol. It can take the form of the great houses of the Anglo-Irish landlord class, like Coole Park or the Gore-Booth's Lissadell in Co. Sligo. Sometimes it is the 'grey / Eighteenth century houses' of Dublin in 'Easter 1916'. But the most powerful and rich symbol for Yeats is his Norman Tower at Thoor Ballylee in Co. Galway.

Yeats bought and started to rebuild this tower in 1915, but he invested more than money and labour in it. He also invested his imagination. The tower became a major component of his mythology, its 'winding ancient stair' in 'A Dialogue of Self and Soul' a symbol of the ascent that the soul has to make to gain a vantage on history. It became too a symbol of the gyres of that history itself. From its battlements he stares at the surrounding countryside in 'The Tower'. He sees 'Phantoms of Hatred and of the Heart's Fullness and of the Coming Emptiness' in 'Meditations in Time of Civil War'. We see his shadow sitting at its window in 'The Phases of the Moon'. Its broken and decaying roof becomes the image of a time 'half dead at the top' in 'Blood and the Moon'. Here he 'declare[s] this tower . . . my symbol', imagining its stairs trodden by his masterful Anglo-Irish forbears Goldsmith, Swift, Berkeley and Burke, and its survival a testimony to the brutal mastery of the conquering settler population in Ireland from the Normans until today:

> Blessed be this place,
> More blessed still this tower;
> A bloody, arrogant power
> Rose out of the race
> Uttering, mastering it,
> Rose like these walls from these
> Storm-beaten cottages –

> In mockery I have set
> A powerful emblem up,
> And sing it rhyme upon rhyme
> In mockery of a time
> Half dead at the top.

He goes on to recall some of the acts of blood that may have been committed within its walls, as the bastion of one occupying power after another. 'There, on blood-saturated ground, have stood / Soldier, assassin, executioner', so that there is 'Odour of blood on the ancestral stair'. Yeats is saying here that 'every modern nation' is founded in blood, and he goes on to ask whether they are also 'Half dead at the top' before concluding that 'power, / Like everything that has the stain of blood, / [is] A property of the living'.

In 'Meditations' the tower is revisited by that violence, as the Irish Civil War of 1922–3 brings first 'An affable Irregular [IRA soldier] . . . cracking jokes of civil war' and then government troops, 'A brown Lieutenant and his men, / Half dressed in national uniform', to his door, as well as stories of horror and atrocity on both sides.

Yeats liked to think of his tower as, like Irish history, haunted, and in 'The Tower' he fantasised this in terms of violent images from its medieval and Norman past, as if the tower were itself some repository of the 'Great Memory':

> Before that ruin came, for centuries,
> Rough men-at-arms, cross-gartered to the knees
> Or shod in iron, climbed the narrow stairs,
> And certain men-at-arms there were
> Whose images, in the Great Memory stored,
> Come with loud cry and panting breast
> To break upon a sleeper's rest
> While their great wooden dice beat on the board.

For Yeats, then, the tower becomes a symbol of Ireland, haunted by its murderous past. In choosing to rebuild it, he is choosing too to accept that Ireland as his burden and responsibility. At the end of this poem he not only embraces this inherited world but transmits it to his spiritual heirs by writing a will.

3.6 THE ANTI-SELF OR MASK

We can see how Yeats's theory of the symbol has practical effects when we consider what he said about the role of the symbol in shaping not only the individual but the collective consciousness. Just as the individual could be unified by finding the symbol which made sense of his life, so Ireland itself would be unified only when it discovered that myth, image or symbol that summed up all its possibilities, past and present. This symbol would arise from, or be entered in, 'the book of the people'. It would have to be one that challenges a people to strive to their utmost. It should set a task which is only just possible by the greatest straining of their abilities. Anything less would be unworthy of them. Anything more, by being impossible of fulfilment, would encourage only despair:

> Nations, races, and individual men are unified by an image, or bundle of images, symbolical or evocative of the state of mind, which is of all states of mind not impossible, the most difficult to that man, race or nation; because only the greatest obstacle that can be contemplated without despair, rouses the will to full intensity. (*Autobiographies*, p. 194)

For Ireland, according to Yeats, it was the tragic heroism of the solitary Charles Stewart Parnell which offered this challenge. Parnell becomes a symbol, representing to Ireland everything that it was not but could, by conscious choice, become.

This alternative or antithetical self Yeats called the 'anti-self'. As he writes in 'The Trembling of the Veil' (*Autobiographies*, p. 195):

> I had seen Ireland in my own time turn from the bragging rhetoric and gregarious humour of O'Connell's generation and school, and offer herself to the solitary and proud Parnell as to her anti-self, buskin following hard on sock, and I had begun to hope, or to half-hope, that we might be the first in Europe to seek unity as deliberately as it had been sought by the theologian, poet, sculptor, architect, from the eleventh to the thirteenth century.

As far as Yeats was concerned, Ireland betrayed the image of its greatness by rejecting Parnell, preferring instead to lapse back into the inferior nationalism represented by O'Connell, all wheedling and bullying and what 'Easter 1916' called 'casual comedy'. The 'sock' of the low-bred comedian is here contrasted with the 'buskin' or high-heeled boot worn by the hero in Greek tragedy. The Greek tragic actor also wore a mask and, Yeats believed, the assumption of the mask allowed an escape from personality into the impersonal realm where 'unity of being' was possible.

To enter into tragic grandeur, the modern poet and hero must assume the mask of their anti-selves, of all that in life they are not. Wearing the mask, the individual can act parts totally the opposite of his or her normal self. Yeats found these ideas confirmed by the aristocratic, impersonal and stylised drama of the Japanese Noh plays, whose actors also wore masks and moved with carefully choreographed gestures. Among 'subject-ive men', he says in 'The Trembling', the thoughts which sustain them in defeat, or give victory, are those in which there is:

> . . . an intellectual daily re-creation of all that exterior fate snatches away, and so that fate's antithesis; while what I have called 'the Mask' is an emotional antithesis to all that comes out of their internal nature. We begin to live when we have conceived life as tragedy. (C, p. 334)

In 'A General Introduction for my Work' (C, p. 255), Yeats spelt out how this relates to his theory of art. 'A poet', he says, 'writes always of his personal life', but 'he never speaks directly as to someone at the breakfast table, there is always a phantasma-goria.' By this word he means a fantasy, or story-telling element. For the poet in the poem, even when he seems most himself, 'is never the bundle of accident and incoherence that sits down to breakfast'. Instead, 'he has been reborn as an idea, something intended, complete' – as, that is, his anti-self, who has a wholeness and unity of being lacking in the real-life poet. The personal has thus become impersonal, assuming the mask of art. The reborn self 'is more type than man, more passion than type. He is Lear, Romeo, Oedipus, Tiresias; he has stepped out of a play, and even the woman he loves is Rosalind, Cleopatra, never the Dark Lady' of his personal life. Even when she is still called Maud Gonne rather than Helen, one might add, she is like the Maud transfigured into a 'human, superhuman' image in metal in 'A Bronze Head'.

3.7 IRELAND, BYZANTIUM AND ENGLAND

ROME/ROMAN EMPIRE.

In art, then, the poet can hammer his thoughts into a unity missing from the realm of real life, as a nation or a people can forge a unity out of the disparate images of their history. For Yeats, the antithesis of modern Ireland may be the heroic age of the Celtic past, or it may be medieval Byzantium. 'Sailing to Byzantium' contrasts the time-bound world of Ireland and nature (with its 'dying generations') with the world of Byzantium and art, whose 'Monuments of unageing intellect' celebrate 'the artifice of eternity'.

This argument is best glossed by his comments in *A Vision*:

> I think that in early Byzantium, maybe never before or since in recorded history, religious, aesthetic and practical life were one, that architects and artificers . . . spoke to the multitude and the few alike. The painter, the mosaic worker, the worker in gold or silver, the illuminator of sacred books, were almost impersonal, almost perhaps without the consciousness of individual design, absorbed in their subject-matter and that the vision of a whole people. (1925, pp. 190–1; 1937, 279–80)

Ireland, he believes, will gain its unity when all the forms of its life and culture converge in 'the vision of a whole people'. This will come only when Ireland renounces the dominance of England over all aspects of its life. For Ireland's antithesis, in a negative, destructive way, may also be England.

Yeats believed that such unified communities still survived only in the semi-legendary west of Ireland – communities contrasted with those of an England where money-grubbing, capitalist values had set class against class, creating a democracy founded on either giving in to or manipulating the mob. As he wrote in the beautiful, almost convincing prose of 'The Galway Plains':

> There is still in truth upon those great level plains a people, a community bound together by imaginative possessions, by stories and poems which have grown out of its own life, and by a past of great passions which can still waken the heart to imaginative action. . . . Does not the greatest poetry always require a people to listen to it? England or any other country which takes its tunes from the great cities and gets its taste from schools and not from old custom may have a mob, but it cannot have a people. . . . The poet must always prefer the community where the perfected minds express the people, to a community that is vainly seeking to copy the perfected minds. . . . A people alone are a great river; and that is why I am persuaded that where a people has died, a nation is about to die. (C, p. 129)

3.8   ART, ARISTOCRACY AND DEMOCRACY

The passage above brings together a cluster of ideas which are always interrelated in Yeats's work. Yeats believed in the values of a hierarchical, ordered society in which a cultural and political aristocracy gave leadership and dignity to a people who respected and served them. In such a society, economic and political inequality would be unimportant compared with the sense of unity and wholeness derived from sharing a common culture and set of values. This right-wing idea of society is usually referred to as that of the 'corporate state' or the 'organic community'.

Any aristocracy which does not 'express the people', Yeats suggests in 'The Galway Plains', but like the English elite merely offers perfected norms of taste to be copied by the multitude, is cut off from its strengths. The role of the artist, he proposes, is to try to renew the old links between aristocracy and people by creating a culture in which all alike could share. It was in the hope that an Irish cultural renaissance might be able to restore such a connection that Yeats threw himself into trying to create a 'People's Theatre' at the Abbey Theatre in Dublin.

Yeats found that it was not as easy as he had imagined to bring about such a renaissance. Indeed, some of his finest poems express, not the organic sensibility of a united Ireland, but the stress and strain of a society riven by class and faction, a country as much under the rule of mob and demagogue as England. When Sir Hugh Lane's offer of his Impressionist paintings to the City of Dublin was turned down by councillors and businessmen who thought them not worth the cost of building a decent gallery, Yeats was provoked to write a poem with perhaps the longest title in the English language – its very prosiness spelling out his contempt for such philistines: 'To a Wealthy Man who promised a Second Subscription to the Dublin Municipal Gallery if it were proved the People wanted Pictures'.

The poem makes it clear that it is the venal, commercial mentality of the Irish middle classes, together with the indifference of the lower classes, which are to blame. His anger is summed up by the insulting, almost racialist gibes about a 'blind and ignorant town' that thinks only money matters. Yeats contrasted these attitudes with the noble values of the Italian Renaissance, where the Dukes of Ferrara and Urbino patronised the arts without caring for profit or the mob's opinions. Cosimo de Medici, Yeats suggests, was 'Indifferent how the rancour ran' when he was driven out of Florence, turning his mind at once to plans for the San Marco Library. The same can hardly be said of Yeats, whose clearly genuine rancour here only just redeems a fine poem from mere snobbery, leaving the Paudeens (an insulting term for Irishmen, derived from the Gaelic version of Paddy or Patrick) to 'play at pitch and toss' in a culturally vacuous Dublin.

The same rancour fuels poems such as 'To a Friend whose Work has come to Nothing' and 'On those that hated "The Playboy of the Western World", 1907', a poem about the 'Abbey Riots' against John Synge's supposed 'slander' of Irish womanhood (see Chapter 2, 'Maud Gonne'):

> Once, when midnight smote the air,
> Eunuchs ran through Hell and met
> On every crowded street to stare
> Upon great Juan riding by:

>   Even like these to rail and sweat
>   Staring upon his sinewy thigh.

Yeats's language is explicitly sexual, seeing the crisis focused by
the play as that diagnosed in James Joyce's almost contemporary
novel, *A Portrait of the Artist as a Young Man*, which had shown
Ireland to be under the thumb of sexual as well as political
repression. Nationalist journalists such as Arthur Griffith, who
led the clamour for Synge's blood, are seen as the eunuchs
whose voices are made shrill by political agitation.

A diary extract in *Estrangement* makes it clear that this is more
than the expression of personal chagrin. It is, in fact, the key
to Yeats's later political attitudes, when he turned from the
sentimental socialism of William Morris, and the passionate
nationalism of O'Leary, to the anti-democratic rant of his later
years. 'The root of it all', he wrote,

> is that the political class in Ireland – the lower-middle class
> from whom the patriotic associations have drawn their journal-
> ists and their leaders for the last ten years – have suffered
> through the cultivation of hatred as the one energy of their
> movement, a deprivation which is the intellectual equivalent
> to a certain surgical operation. Hence the shrillness of their
> voices. They contemplate all creative power as the eunuchs
> contemplate Don Juan as he passes through Hell on the white
> horse. (*Autobiographies*, p. 486)

Yeats returned to the Abbey episode late in life for one of his
most poignant poems of recollection, 'Beautiful Lofty Things'.
The poem offers a host of possibilities forfeited by modern
Ireland, all images of spiritual aristocracy confronting a degraded
world. The sense of irreparable loss is communicated by the
way in which Yeats piles up a list of instances without ever
letting them issue in a main verb, to culminate in the one, still
verbless concluding phrase: 'All the Olympians; a thing never
known again'. The list ends with the image of Maud Gonne's
'straight back and arrogant head' waiting for a train. It carries
lightning profiles of nationalist leaders and Lady Gregory's aged
dignity. But it is surely the sharp sarcasm of Yeats's father which
animates the whole, adding a peculiar colour to all its other

instances, manipulating jingoistic phrases with an impeccable theatrical timing which Yeats's poem emulates:

My father upon the Abbey stage, before him a raging crowd:
'This Land of Saints,' and then as the applause died out,
'Of plaster saints'; his beautiful mischievous head thrown back.

For Yeats, democracy is the politics of 'plaster saints'. True art could thrive, he thought, only in a society in which the exceptional individual, in art and politics alike, is revered by a people that knows what is truly valuable and cherishes its 'beautiful lofty things'.

3.9 POET AND PEOPLE

In 'A General Introduction for my Work' in 1937 (C, pp. 255–69) Yeats wrote of his early desire to emulate the poets of the Young Ireland movement, who 'were not separated individual men; they spoke or tried to speak out of a people to a people; behind them stretched the generations'. 'I wanted', he says, 'to get back to Homer. . . . I wanted to cry as all men cried, to laugh as all men laughed, and the Young Ireland poets when not writing mere politics had the same want, but they did not know that the common and its befitting language is the research of a lifetime and when found may lack popular recognition.'

Here is expressed the whole dilemma of Yeats, both as poet and political thinker. Wanting to speak from and to a people, he finds that all he values 'lack[s] popular recognition'. He may use the language of the common people, but this does not guarantee that he can speak to them. They may be too busy fumbling in the greasy till to pay any heed. In the end, in fact, not hostility but indifference is what the Irish artist has suffered from his public.

In *Estrangement* Yeats acknowledged as much. Indeed, it is to this, he suggests, that we can trace his theory of the mask, or antithetical self, an heroic and impersonal 'cold eye' turning in contempt on a foul world:

To oppose the new ill-breeding of Ireland, which may in a

few years destroy all that has given Ireland a distinguished name in the world . . . I can only set up a secondary or interior personality created out of the tradition of myself, and the personality (alas, only possible to me in my writings) must be always gracious and simple. (*Autobiographies*, p. 463)

The first task for the poet was to create his own antithetical self, something 'always gracious and simple' in contrast with the complexity and confusion of his actual life. He could do this partly by modelling himself on Ireland's heroic figures.

'Everything calls up its contrary', he wrote in 'First Principles' in 1904:

I do not believe it a national prejudice that makes me believe we are harder, a more masterful race than the comfortable English of our time, and that this comes from an essential nearness to reality of those few scattered people who have the right to call themselves the Irish race. It is only in the exceptions, in the few minds where the flame has burnt, as it were, pure, that one can see the permanent character of a race. If one remembers the men who have dominated Ireland for the last hundred and fifty years, one can understand that it is strength of personality, the individualising quality in a man, that stirs Irish imagination most deeply in the end. There is scarcely a man who has led the Irish people, at any time, who may not give some day to a great writer precisely that symbol he may require for the expression of himself. (C, p. 135)

Major Robert Gregory, in Yeats's elegy for him, is one who burnt with such a flame, as are Lionel Johnson, John Synge and indeed many of the friends Yeats celebrates. Indeed, Yeats seems to have been singularly fortunate in knowing, by his own estimate, virtually every pure gemlike flame in Ireland. At the end of 'The Municipal Gallery Revisited' Yeats contemplates not 'The dead Ireland of my youth' but an imaginary, antithetical country, 'an Ireland / The poets have imagined, terrible and gay'. He asks to be judged not by his books but by the quality of his friends portrayed there:

Ireland's history in their lineaments trace. . . .
And say my glory was I had such friends.

Most of the figures Yeats claims 'have the right to call themselves
the Irish race', as we have already seen (in the first two sections
of Chapter 2), turn out to be members not of the Catholic and
peasant majority, but of the Anglo-Irish Protestant Ascendancy.
Yeats marginalises the true forces that shaped Irish history in
this period, and gives undue prominence to those literary figures
such as Synge and Lady Gregory who contributed to its cultural
revival. For it is in this genteel or artistic elite that he found
Ireland's anti-self, focused most powerfully in the figure of
Parnell, and in those predecessors cited in 'Parnell's Funeral',
Emmet, Fitzgerald, Tone. By contrast, the Catholic leader O'Connell is there spoken of as 'the Great Comedian', in dismissive
tones.

Yeats looked to this lineage for the symbol which would give
him the expression of himself. But he still needed another
component to complete his imagined Ireland. This lay in an
imagined, as opposed to the actual, peasantry. He found it in
that 'race / Passionate and simple like his heart' first revealed to
him by the writings of Synge, as he tells us in stanza IV of 'In
Memory of Major Robert Gregory'.

In 'A People's Theatre' Yeats wrote of his generation's
ambition as 'the making articulate of all the dumb classes each
with its own knowledge of the world, its own dignity, but all
objective with the objectivity of the office and the workshop, of
the newspaper and the street, of mechanism and politics' (C,
pp. 185–6). But such 'objectivity' could not reconcile the heroic
attitudes of an 'Olympian' elite with 'the day's war with every
knave and dolt'.

Yeats's solution was not only to invent an antithetical personality 'out of the tradition of myself'; nor just to create an antithetical
Ireland out of its mythology and romanticised history. To
appreciate such an idea of Ireland, he needed also to forge an
imaginary audience worthy of his art.

In 'The Fisherman', Yeats's audience, Yeats's people and
Yeats's Ireland are all called up and imagined in defiance of any
actual readership and nation. The poem begins with a concessive
conjunction which indicates how much of a fantasy this is:

'Although I can see him still', he says, 'It's long since I began / To call up to the eyes / This wise and simple man.' His fisherman may be presented in coarse detail, down to the quality of his 'grey Connemara cloth', but he is only a figure in the mind. The poet has 'all day . . . looked in the face / What I had hoped 'twould be / To write for my own race / And the reality'. He goes on:

> Maybe a twelvemonth since
> Suddenly I began,
> In scorn of this audience,
> Imagining a man.

But it is 'the reality' which triumphs in the end. The poet has to admit that the Fisherman, his ideal audience, is 'A man who does not exist, / A man who is but a dream'. What is more, in his absence the poet's own real poems cannot come into existence, remain speculative hopes for the future. The poem ends with a wish that

> . . . Before I am old
> I shall have written him one
> Poem maybe as cold
> And passionate as the dawn.

Like the 'Although' with which the poem opens, these 'maybes' leave us in the realm of unrealised, merely subjunctive hopes. Yeats's vision of Ireland is a double one. On the one hand there are the illusory ideal actors and audience, typified by the Fisherman and the imaginary peasantry of the West, as by his heroic and solitary individuals. On the other hand, there is the actual world of lower–middle-class Dublin where 'the common and its befitting language' are reduced to 'the commonest ear', and a true elite is usurped by the demagogic 'clever man' with 'the catch-cries of the clown'. In such a world, we see 'great Art beaten down'.

Yeats's ideal image of the artist and poet cannot be separated from his ideal images of aristocracy and people. The former are to be the patrons of great art, but the latter are to be its real beneficiaries. The essay 'Poetry and Tradition' sums up the convergence Yeats saw between aristocrat, peasant and poet:

> Three types of men have made all beautiful things. Aristocra-
> cies have made beautiful manners, because their place in the
> world puts them above the fear of life, and the countrymen
> have made beautiful stories and beliefs, because they have
> nothing to lose and so do not fear, and the artists have
> made all the rest, because Providence has filled them with
> recklessness. All these look backward to a long tradition, for,
> being without fear, they have held to whatever pleased them.
> (C, p. 160)

When the artist can forge a united audience out of his fellow
artists, his patrons, and the peasantry, great art will no longer
be beaten down. The artist will have hammered his thoughts
into a unity. And he will have mastered Ireland in all her moods.
That is, an authentic Ireland will have been forged which is a
political and a cultural unity.

3.10 THE HERO

From his earliest years Yeats was preoccupied with the idea of
the heroic individual. In the first poetry of the 'Celtic Twilight'
it was the heroic figures of ancient Irish myth who obsessed
him, Oisin and Cuchulain. Later, it is such figures of his
own day as Parnell and Major Robert Gregory, the right-wing
politician Kevin O'Higgins, and others. At the very end of his
life, in 'The Circus Animals' Desertion', he remembers the 'old
themes' of his youth as 'allegorical dreams, / Vain gaiety, vain
battles, vain repose, / Themes of the embittered heart'. Although
his poems and plays, he suggests, had a hidden, allegorical
or emblematic significance, it was really the heroic figures
themselves, incident and action and revelation, which held his
imagination:

> Character isolated by a deed
> To engross the present and dominate memory.

> Players and painted stage took all my love,
> And not those things that they were emblems of.

Yeats's heroic figures are important primarily as instances of character revealed by a single action which sums up their identity and significance. In 'An Irish Airman Foresees his Death', Major Robert Gregory at a moment of self-recognition becomes a representative of all such individuals isolated in the extremity of choice. The poem is a *dramatic monologue*, words put into the mouth of one who fought and died as a pilot in the British airforce in the Great War.

For Yeats, the heroism of this man is self-sufficient. It does not serve some ulterior cause, law or duty or fame, for 'Those that I fight I do not hate, / Those that I guard I do not love'. Gregory thinks of himself not as an Englishman but as an Irishman, with his loyalty to the country and poor people of Kiltartan, near his mother's estate at Coole Park. His character is isolated by a deed which is its own justification:

> A lonely impulse of delight
> Drove to this tumult in the clouds.

The poem itself, in its careful balancing of lines, clauses, phrases and words, enacts Gregory's own moral deliberations, and the only lines which depart from this proliferation of antithetical constructions are the two quoted, driving out of the carefully balanced world of ordinary human priorities into the singularity of impulse and delight.

Loneliness is a feature of Yeats's heroes. Their heroism sets them apart and distinguishes them from the public men and the cheering crowds. In his great elegy 'In Memory of Major Robert Gregory' Yeats lists a collection of such exceptional individuals he has been privileged to know, the poet Lionel Johnson, the playwright John Synge, his horse-riding uncle George Pollexfen. What makes them stand out is the extremism of their commitment to life. For the purpose of his elegy, and not without some strain, Yeats proposes that Gregory himself epitomised such an intensity. He uses a metaphor which is recurrent in his verse for that moment of intensity in which time is consumed, rendered meaningless and irrelevant – the flaring up of a flame which leaves nothing behind:

> Some burn damp faggots, others may consume
> The entire combustible world in one small room
> As though dried straw, and if we turn about
> The bare chimney is gone black out
> Because the work had finished in that flare.

The 'flare' is the same as the lonely delight which 'brings all to mind', concentrates it in a single moment of intense excitement. As Yeats says in the second of 'Two Songs from a Play':

> Everything that man esteems
> Endures a moment or a day . . .
> Whatever flames upon the night
> Man's own resinous heart has fed.

In 'Easter 1916' the uprising itself has transformed men who were once ordinary, mundane, even ludicrous, into heroes with an almost supernatural aura, converted a world of 'casual comedy' where the 'motley' of the clown is worn, into one of tragic grandeur. One of these rebels, executed by the English, had been an enemy of Yeats's – John McBride, the husband of Maud Gonne. But now, he says, he realised that he had merely 'dreamed' him 'A drunken vainglorious lout'. In reality, he has been 'Transformed utterly'. The 'vivid faces' among the 'Polite meaningless words' have been vindicated. Such heroes, by their deeds and deaths, have entered a mythical realm.

Yeats deploys the language of *enchantment* to describe this transformation. Their hearts, committed to a single purpose – Irish independence – have been enchanted to a stone. It may be 'excess of love/Bewildered them till they died.' But such excess takes them into a realm outside the ordinary ('grey/Eighteenth century houses' and 'ignorant good-will'), to the 'dream' world of Irish folk legend, along with the heroes of the ancient past. Thus Ireland and history too have been transfigured by their sacrifice (Easter is a significant occasion here): 'All changed, changed utterly:/A terrible beauty is born'.

At the end of his life, in 'The Statues', Yeats spelt out this mythical transformation in reference to Padraic Pearse (see Chapter 2.5). Yeats's rhetoric overcomes the possibly comic location for this heroic act – the Dublin Post Office – by calling up the world of Irish myth as he suggests the rebels imperiously did: 'When Pearse summoned Cuchulain to his side, / What stalked through the Post Office?' Without saying what does stalk, he is carried forward on the strength of his rhetorical question to generalise a distinction between 'We Irish, born into that ancient sect' and the 'filthy modern tide' upon which Ireland is wrecked.

The contrast, as always, is between the commonplace world of history, and a timeless order of heroism in which greatness flames upon the night. For, as he says of the boys and girls 'pale from the imagined love / Of solitary beds' in the first stanza, he knows 'That passion could bring character enough'. Passion, intensity, ecstasy even, are the characteristics of the hero in Yeats's thought. His heroes are entranced, enchanted, transfigured, entering into that 'Heroic reverie' which is contrasted with the mockery of clown and knave in 'A Bronze Head'.

In a word drawn from the German philosopher Friedrich Nietzsche, Yeats speaks of this ecstasy as a kind of *gaiety*. In 'Lapis Lazuli', for example, he speaks of the 'tragic play' of modern history, an unreal performance. But, at the moment of crisis, this theatrical strutting is transfigured into real heroism:

> Yet they, should the last scene be there . . .
> Do not break up their lines to weep.
> They know that Hamlet and Lear are gay;
> Gaiety transfiguring all that dread.
> All men have aimed at, found and lost;
> Black out; Heaven blazing into the head:
> Tragedy wrought to its uttermost.

These figures have been 'reborn as an idea, something intended, complete', or, in the words of 'Poetry and Tradition' (*C*, pp. 160–1) they are 'reborn in gaiety'. They have made themselves into their anti-selves, assumed the tragic mask. Yeats in 1936 refused to include the poets of the Great War in his *Oxford Book of Modern Verse* on the grounds that such poets lacked this tragic, heroic sense, instead dealing in pathos and pity: 'passive suffering is

not a theme for poetry. In all the great tragedies, tragedy is a
joy to the man who dies; in Greece the tragic chorus danced'
(*C*, p. 234).

3.11 BEAUTY, WOMAN, CARNAL KNOWLEDGE

If Yeats's men are heroes, his women are beautiful, even when
'skeleton-gaunt' in old age, for beauty to Yeats is close to heroism
and is associated with dignity, a sense of innate superiority to
the common mob, and a defiant self-assurance. 'To a Young
Beauty' spells this out with an opening address to the girl as a
'Dear fellow artist'. He sees in authentic beauty the same reward
for effort that the poet has, as the result of what 'The Phases of
the Moon' calls 'mysterious wisdom won by toil'. 'Adam's
Curse' had been an early statement of the theme, which opens
with a memory of sitting together with a beautiful woman at
one summer's end:

> I said, 'A line will take us hours maybe;
> Yet if it does not seem a moment's thought,
> Our stitching and unstitching has been naught.
> Better go down upon your marrow-bones
> And scrub a kitchen pavement, or break stones
> Like an old pauper . . .'

To write poetry 'Is to work harder than all these' and yet be
despised as 'an idler' by the practical people of the world.
Significantly Yeats's analogies are with two forms of unglamor-
ous but traditionally 'female' labour, stitching and scrubbing, as
well as with the hard labour of the poor. But the beautiful
woman replies out of an instinctive sympathy:

> 'To be born woman is to know –
> Although they do not talk of it at school –
> That we must labour to be beautiful.'

'Adam's Curse' is the curse imposed by God for eating the
apple of knowledge: 'by the sweat of thy brow shalt thou labour'.
The poem ends on a 'weary-hearted' note that returns it to the

langorous rhythms of the Celtic Twilight, but its opening, vigorous metre had established an abiding preoccupation of Yeats's: that all beauty, whether in art or women, is won by 'hard labouring', not acquired casually or idly. Love without labour is thus an 'idle trade'.

'To a Young Beauty' takes up the idea of 'trade' by speaking of beauty as a 'wage' for effort. It also takes up the hostility to schoolroom knowledge, which Yeats thought teaches us nothing, by contrasting with it the mirror in which the young woman practises as the real school of learning. 'Michael Robartes and the Dancer' turns into a dramatic confrontation between the sexes, in dialogue, on this very point. Robartes equates thinking with 'Opinion', something Yeats despised. In 'A Prayer for my Daughter' Yeats wishes that she will 'think opinions are accursed' and goes on to ask, thinking of Maud Gonne's politics:

> Have I not seen the loveliest woman born
> Out of the mouth of Plenty's horn,
> Because of her opinionated mind
> Barter that horn and every good
> By quiet natures understood
> For an old bellows full of angry wind?

The word 'barter' associates 'opinions' with 'trade'. Ideas are exchanged in the market-place, they come and go, transitory possessions, rather than being the deepest and most integral part of one's nature. In this poem, Michael Robartes claims that 'Opinion is not worth a rush'. But he himself is full of opinions. He refers to a painting in which St George kills the dragon to rescue a lady, which he sees as an image of rescuing her from her own thinking. If, instead of thinking, she turned her eyes upon her mirror, her lover thinks she 'on the instant would grow wise'. Her reply is shrewd and terse: 'You mean they argued'. She is not fooled by his argumentative and opinionated dismissal of arguments and opinions. He advises her, patronisingly, to

> bear in mind your lover's wage
> Is what your looking-glass can show.

She is 'learned' enough to know that all this philosophy and

art history is really about seduction. There is considerable irony
here. The wage, we note, is not that of the beauty, but of the
lover, though whether he is drawing it or paying it is unclear.
This is a very male-centred way of seeing things, and is
vigorously rebutted by the girl's single-line question: 'May I not
put myself to college?' Not only is she asserting her independence and self-direction here, she is somewhat sarcastically
pointing out that Robartes seems to assume she needs his
permission to do anything. His dismissive reply perhaps unwit-
tingly acknowledges that the Greek god of wisdom was in fact
a goddess. The rhetorical command, 'go pluck Athena by the
hair', also calls attention to what for Yeats is always a powerful
symbol of female beauty, the hair, demeans Athena by this
petty act, and leads on to a more overwhelming assault on the
female. A woman's place, it seems, is on her back, and the best
knowledge she can acquire is carnal knowledge, that which she
learns in bed. Robartes' language gets more explicitly sexual
here:

> For what mere book can grant a knowledge
> With an impassioned gravity
> Appropriate to that beating breast,
> That vigorous thigh, that dreaming eye?
> And may the devil take the rest.

With impressive persistence, the girl refuses this reduction of
her to her sexual features, with a curt question for question:
'And must no beautiful woman be / Learned like a man?' He
replies by invoking the beautiful bodies painted by Veronese
and Michael Angelo, as if these were sufficient 'proof' of his
argument 'That all must come to sight and touch' – that is, that
the 'true' knowledge is a carnal, sensual one. He raises, too, the
question of 'rule' as something physically founded in the
'supernatural right' of male sinew. Her reply ('I have heard
said / There is great danger in the body') is at once sceptical and
a little playfully prudish. She is reproaching him, in a way, for
talking dirty. She invokes, we later see, ironically, that patriarchal authority which says she must keep herself pure. His
reply is by way of a riddle that also invokes male authority in
the form of religion:

> Did God in portioning wine and bread
> Give man His thought or His mere body?

He now, having professed to despise book-learning, invokes it
to 'prove' his case: 'It follows from this Latin text', he says, that
beautiful women can teach men, 'if they/Will banish every
thought' – unless they think it with their bodies. The looking-
glass is thus once again contrasted with 'school'.

The girl has the last, ambiguous word. She seems to be giving
in to his argument, with the remark 'They say such different
things at school'. But she is not just overawed by his arguments
against her judgement. She has also led him on to admit his
interest in her, to engage in this forceful wooing. The clinching
irony, of course, is that all Robartes' bookish and theoretical
arguments for this carnal or 'bodily' knowledge count for nothing
against the simple fact that, as a dancer, she knows it all already.
For the one thing a dancer has to know is how to think with
her body, otherwise she will never put a foot right.

Far from being a poem which exposits Yeats's male chauvinist
ideas about the subordination of women to men, the poem is a
genuinely dramatic, and even comic, enactment of the perennial
guerrilla war of the sexes, in which no battle is ever final, and
apparent surrender can be victory. The girl, after all, reserves
her judgement. She doesn't say: 'Very true O master'. What she
does is to contrast the two knowledges and arguments, with a
sly indication that she is actually going to try both. What might
have been a distasteful exercise in patriarchal bullying thus
becomes a graceful and witty tussle over issues which are at
once serious and comical, tragic and banal. Yeats's use of
dramatic dialogue, the form of the poem itself, we might say
deconstructs the ideology, the 'opinions', it is supposed to
advance.

3.12 PHILOSOPHERS AND DANCERS

Frank Kermode, in *Romantic Image*, has explored some of the
meanings of the image of the dancer which is a recurrent (and
nearly always female) figure in Yeats's poetry. 'Among School
Children' is an extremely complex poem which takes up many
of the themes already discussed.

The poem centres on a contrast between the two knowing, abstract and concrete. In a letter to Lad written three weeks before he died, Yeats wrote:

> I am happy, and I think full of an energy, of an energy I had despaired of. It seems to me that I have found what I wanted. When I try to put all into a phrase I say, 'Man can embody truth but he cannot know it'. I must embody it in the completion of my life. The abstract is not life and everywhere draws out its contradictions. You can refute Hegel but not the Saint or the Song of Sixpence.

This poem sets out to refute not the philosopher Hegel, but his philosophical predecessors starting with Plato, by contrasting their interest in the abstract, 'the ghostly paradigm of things', with the embodied forms of the dancer and the tree. For Plato a particular thing is only significant as the embodiment of a 'paradigm', the abstract *form* which lies behind and generates it. Nature is composed of multitudes of particular things, but these things are mortal, the 'dying generations' of 'Sailing to Byzantium'. All particular trees and dancers come into and pass out of existence, but the idea, or 'paradigm' of tree, human form, and dance remain, to be embodied in new particular trees and dancers.

This poem is much concerned with Yeats's own sense of impending death, now that he is sixty, to be replaced by the children in the classroom, who will grow old and die in their turn, as stanza V makes apparent, to be replaced by others. Maud Gonne, the youthful 'Ledaean body' remembered in stanza II, has also now turned into the hollow-cheeked old woman of stanza IV. Her 'present image', in memory, is partly mocked by the embodied image that 'stands before [him] as a living child'.

This contrast between abstract paradigm and embodied particular is found at the level of learning too. In the classroom, the children are taught generalities, reading, writing, singing, 'In the best modern way'. But all the time, they have a different kind of knowledge, revealed by that 'momentary wonder' in their eyes. For Yeats, this is a more authentic knowledge, usually lost in growing up, the knowledge of the imagination. As a poet, however, he himself still possesses it, for by stanza III he is no longer just 'A sixty-year-old smiling public man' but one who, dreaming of his youthful past and Maud Gonne, has himself returned to the realm of 'wonder'. Such a way of knowing can drive the heart wild, unlike the neatness and regularity of classroom knowledge, and it can only be encompassed by the embodied images of art. But art can glorify old age. By comparison, he feels himself no more than 'a comfortable kind of old scarecrow'.

This leads him to question the value of life, if nothing endures. Would a young mother, he wonders in stanza V, consider the pain of childbirth and the struggles of raising children worthwhile, if she could look into the future and see her child as a sixty year old man like himself? It is this almost despairing sense of the transitoriness of life which leads him on to the philosophical speculations of stanza VI.

Something needs to be said about these philosophers, but not much. One should note how much of Yeats's contempt for Plato's 'ideal forms' is revealed by the play of words like 'spume' and 'ghostly'. Aristotle is 'solider' because as a philosopher he was concerned with enumerating and understanding the actual variety and substance of things in the real, not the ideal world. As the schoolmaster of Alexander the Great, he also had a very practical grasp of how even god-kings need to be disciplined when young, if they are to learn anything. (As I explained in Chapter 1, the 'taws' was a leather belt used in Irish schools for instilling 'the best modern ways'). Pythagoras, enquirer into mathematical harmonies and into measurements of the musical scale, also speculated on the transmigration of souls after death. But all these followed a merely abstract knowledge, speculating, like Hegel, about what the stars and the Muses knew instinctively, carelessly and casually. Their philosophies are thus, like the aged Yeats, little more than scarecrows, intended to scare off the thought of death:

> Plato thought nature but a spume that plays
> Upon a ghostly paradigm of things;
> Solider Aristotle played the taws
> Upon the bottom of a king of kings;
> World-famous golden-thighed Pythagoras

Fingered upon a fiddle-stick or strings
What a star sang and careless Muses heard:
Old clothes upon old sticks to scare a bird.

Both nuns and mothers worship images,
But those the candles light are not as those
That animate a mother's reveries,
But keep a marble or a bronze repose.
And yet they too break hearts – O Presences
That passion, piety or affection knows,
And that all heavenly glory symbolise –
O self-born mockers of man's enterprise;

Labour is blossoming or dancing where
The body is not bruised to pleasure soul,
Nor beauty born out of its own despair,
Nor blear-eyed wisdom out of midnight oil.
O chestnut tree, great rooted blossomer,
Are you the leaf, the blossom or the bole?
O body swayed to music, O brightening glance,
How can we know the dancer from the dance?

Against such abstract knowledge, Yeats in stanza VII sets the concrete embodied 'images' worshipped by nuns and mothers – whether the marble and bronze statuary of religious art or the 'living child' upon the lap. Yeats now here develops his ideas about the images of art, the 'Presences' known, not to the intellect but to intuition, to 'passion, piety or affection'. This is a different kind of knowing, and these images, while they 'symbolise' 'heavenly glory' also abide on earth. They are made by and reflect on 'man's enterprise', but they transcend and outlive their human makers, becoming 'self-born'.

In the same way, we could read Yeats's poem without knowing anything about its author, even his name, let alone his biography. One of the deepest anxieties this poem records is the author's own sense that his poems will outlive him as the paintings of the Italian Quattrocento outlive both their makers and their models. In this way, for each new generation, the works of art they admire seem to be 'self-born'.

The poet now addresses the images of art directly, turning to consider the relation between the coldness and aloofness of art and the warmth and passion of the world of living, organic things it represents. 'Labour', whether the labour of the artist or of the mother in childbirth, will come 'as naturally as the leaves to a tree' only when the division of soul and body, abstract and concrete, is overcome, when wisdom is acquired not by abstract mental effort, burning the midnight oil, but from a joyous instinctive knowledge like that of the tree, which does not have to take thought to throw up its leaves and blossoms from its roots. The dancer becomes a human image of this joyous knowing. She has had to put herself to school to acquire the perfect knowledge of the dance which now seems to come effortlessly, without thought.

As the last rhetorical question insists, there is no way of separating the dancer from the dance. The *form* of the dance can only be seen when a particular person dances it. Similarly, the woman is only a dancer while she is dancing. Her image becomes that embodied, energetic truth which cannot be refuted, while the static scarecrows of philosophy never actually find that which they look for. Even Pythagoras, who seems to know so much about music, only knows it as an abstract pattern, while the stars can sing with an unselfconscious felicity denied him.

But it is not in this ecstatic highflown image that Yeats's method is best revealed, but in an earlier image. In stanza II Yeats speaks of that moment when, hearing from the young Maud Gonne of some 'trivial event' in her childhood which made that day a 'tragedy', it seemed that their 'two natures blent / Into a sphere from youthful sympathy, / Or else, to alter Plato's parable, / Into the yolk and white of the one shell.'

For Plato and Pythagoras, the geometric figure of the sphere, in its self-bounded and mathematical harmony, was a symbol of perfection. Furthermore, in Plato's *Symposium* we read that man and woman were once united in perfection like a sphere, but fell apart, and now spend their lives searching through the world for the other half who will restore their unity. Yeats takes this rather abstract idea of unity and sexual perfection, the sphere, and gives it a concrete embodiment as 'the yolk and white of the one shell'.

Since Leda gave birth to Helen from an egg, this is almost a joke at the expense of the 'daughters of the swan'. More

significantly, perhaps, the oval shape of an egg falls aw
spherical perfection. But what it loses in perfection it
substance, no longer a 'ghostly paradigm' but a nourishing ana
solid material thing, and, what is more, a thing which belongs
to the order of generation, since the egg is the carrier of the
biological 'form' of the bird into the next generation. Yeats's
poem thus confirms, concretely, in the 'embodied truth' of its
imagery the argument it sets out to explore. One might say it
dances its truth, rather than simply setting it out as an abstract
argument which, like Hegel, could be refuted.

3.13 FOLLY AND MADNESS

The idea of a carnal, bodily knowledge is linked for Yeats with
the idea that we learn from folly and derangement. 'A Prayer
for Old Age' puts this with characteristic pungency:

> God guard me from those thoughts men think
> In the mind alone;
> He that sings a lasting song
> Thinks in a marrow-bone.

Such 'knowledge' requires the readiness to be a fool. As Blake
said, if the fool will persist in his folly he will become wise. In
this late poem Yeats prays 'That I may seem, though I die old, / A
foolish, passionate man'. If one is not prepared to take risks, to
appear ludicrous, to put one's foot in it and follow the foolish
impulses of passion, one will never acquire true wisdom. In a
remarkable sequence, the 'Crazy Jane' poems, Yeats sets up a
series of dramatic encounters between the mad old woman,
Crazy Jane, and various representatives of sober authority,
repectability, middle-class caution.

In 'Crazy Jane Talks with the Bishop' the representative of
Church and Morality seems at first to have the last word. This
woman, who has led a licentious life, is now old and withered,
her breasts 'flat and fallen now', and her 'veins must soon be
dry'. His advice, therefore, to 'Live in a heavenly mansion, / Not
in some foul sty' sounds reasonable. Even now, however, Jane
is not prepared to exercise prudence. For her, fair and foul need

each other – a truth that once learned can never be denied by bed or grave. This knowledge combines pride and humiliation. 'The heart's pride' is only 'Learned in bodily lowliness'.

Yeats's sense of the dignity of the body and its functions and needs is here compressed into the most powerful image of all. His frank language is a testimony to the power of his vision of carnality, taking up even the word 'stiff', allowing for the pun on 'whole', aware of the triple meaning of 'pitched' (pitched down, set up – the lurking pun on 'tent' – and defiled with pitch). Wholeness comes from embracing the carnal, she says proudly, not from fleeing it, and this means accepting the squalor of the bodily as the very condition of its beauty:

> 'A woman can be proud and stiff
> When on love intent;
> But love has pitched his mansion in
> The place of excrement;
> For nothing can be sole or whole
> That has not been rent.'

'Crazy Jane Grown Old Looks at the Dancers' carries this further. In the first stanza, as part of the sexual dance, it seems that the 'chosen youth' is about to strangle the dancer with her own hair. In the second stanza, the dancer draws a knife as if to strike her lover dead. Again, Jane cannot intervene, 'For no matter what was said / They had all that had their hate.' As the refrain tells us in each case, 'Love is like the lion's tooth' – is cruel and brutal, and encompasses hatred and murderous thoughts. It is the dance, and not its outcome, that counts.

This may sound like folly, but again what it insists on is the dignity, power and pathos of sexual passion, which in its frenzy overthrows all thoughts of safety and even survival. For Yeats, true knowledge comes from these moments when we let ourselves go, trust to our instincts, and throw caution to the foul winds that blow in another poem, where

> I shudder and I sigh to think
> That even Cicero

And many-minded Homer were
Mad as the mist and snow.

In his own person too, Yeats delighted in the folly and wisdom of age, as in the opening of 'The Wild Old Wicked Man':

'Because I am mad about women
I am mad about the hills'.

In his last poems, stirred to a new vigour by his raging against death, Yeats insists on asking 'Why should not old men be mad?' A 'coarse old man', he insists that any definition of the human must recognise the necessity of 'Bawdy talk'. From his youth onwards, Yeats had learned this lesson the hard way. Initially idealistic and sentimental about love, he had found out the truths of his own mental and physical nature from his passion for Maud Gonne. In 'A Dialogue of Self and Soul' he speaks of this as 'The folly that man does / Or must suffer if he woos / A proud woman not kindred of his soul.' In exploring this folly, he made himself into a great poet.

3.14 UNREQUITED LOVE

Yeats is the great poet of what he calls in 'Presences' 'that monstrous thing / Returned and yet unrequited love'. Early poems such as the paired 'The Pity of Love' and 'The Sorrow of Love' treat the theme with a somewhat abstracted, literary air. In the first, the beloved is a vulnerable waif, threatened by a world full of 'folk who are buying and selling'. In the second, it is the world that is under threat from her 'red mournful lips' which bring with them 'the whole of the world's tears'.

In the revised version of this poem Yeats wrote in 1925 the beloved is ambiguously a *femme fatale*, a woman whose fatal beauty, like Helen of Troy's, drives men to folly and destruction, though the syntax leaves it unclear whether it is girl or world that is 'Doomed like Odysseus and the labouring ships' or 'proud as Priam murdered with his peers' – whether, that is, she is finally cause or victim of misery.

As early as *In the Seven Woods* (1904) Yeats had moved to a more realistic assessment of the complexity of sexual relations, drawing on the disillusionments with Maud Gonne for the rueful worldly wisdom of 'Never Give all the Heart':

> Never give all the heart, for love
> Will hardly seem worth thinking of
> To passionate women if it seem
> Certain, and they never dream
> That it fades out from kiss to kiss.

There is real bitterness in the acerbic aside 'For they, for all smooth lips can say, / Have given their hearts up to the play'. In reacting against an unduly romantic, idealising vision of the woman, one derived in part from the medieval 'courtly love' tradition, the poet adopts a more cynical, combative idea of sexual relations. To love in earnest someone who is only superficially involved is to put oneself at risk, to be 'deaf and dumb and blind with love' when one needs all one's faculties to avoid being taken advantage of. But the potentially cynical tone lapses back into reproachful wistfulness in the closing lines, with the deadbeat rhythms and plaintive whinge: 'He that made this knows all the cost, / For he gave all his heart and lost'. Another poem, 'O Do not Love too Long' tempers its disenchantment with the same almost avuncular urge to give advice:

> But O, in a minute she changed –
> O do not love too long,
> Or you will grow out of fashion
> Like an old song.

By the time of 'Presences' (1915), however, the combination of real and by now varied experience and the maturing of his style have brought an access of emotional power. Much of this is to do with his new-found ability to speak frankly, in a tone that recognises and includes negative feelings, without indulging in the adolescent cynicism with which he had earlier cloaked his disillusion. He no longer simply gloats over having 'seen through' women (when all that had happened was that his own romanticised categories had proved impractical). His new categories for the female principle, summed up in the archetypes 'harlot', 'child' and 'queen', can all be combined in the same women, who can be 'laughing, or timid or wild' by turns. The seductive 'rustle of lace or silken stuff' evokes a contradictory femaleness over which he has no rights and which can move rapidly from vulnerable to ruthless, even turning that very vulnerability into a disturbing power over him.

The poem offers a nightmare vision of female threat. It evokes the supernatural to suggest his terror before the power and strangeness of sexuality, which strikes deep into the self, its violence and destructiveness guarantees of its importance. But it remains ambiguous about this 'supernatural' dimension. 'This night has been so strange', he says, that *it seemed / As if* the hair stood up on my head'. The last line carries the cautious qualification 'it may be'. But from now on Yeats repeatedly uses the hint of the supernatural to explain that mysterious, terrifying power which certain women exercise.

At the end of his life, in 'A Bronze Head', he described a bust of Maud Gonne in the Dublin Municipal Gallery in terms which see this terror shared by the woman herself. Her gaunt, aged image now seems 'Human, super-human, a bird's round eye' which searches the sky but 'finds there nothing to make its terror less'. Even when young, he goes on, although 'a most gentle woman', she had already foreseen this 'vision of terror'. Her wildness called up his: like spoke to like. He still cannot fully comprehend her. But now he sees this strangeness as the condition of her greatness, asking rhetorically 'who can tell / Which of her forms has shown her substance right'.

Lurking behind this complex vision, in which past and present are overlaid, we can detect the three archetypes of 'Presences', harlot, queen and child. None of them, in fact, is sufficient to 'explain' the woman. Her 'substance', what she 'really' is, is only ever glimpsed partially in each of its many passing 'forms'. The supernatural dimension remains only a speculative possibility, one way of interpreting 'the wildness in her' as the repeated 'I thought' and the qualifying conjunctions 'Or else' and 'As though' indicate:

But even at the starting post, all sleek and new,
I saw the wildness in her and I thought
A vision of terror that it must live through

Had shattered her soul. Propinquity had brought
Imagination to that pitch where it casts out
All that is not itself: I had grown wild
And wandered murmuring everywhere, 'my child, my child.'

Or else I thought her supernatural;
As though a sterner eye looked through her eye
On this foul world in its decline and fall.

Her authority over his imagination lies in the fact that there is always about her an excess, a surplus of meaning like that possessed by the symbol, something which cannot be interpreted and pinned down. She remains mysterious and inaccessible, overflowing the 'images' and 'forms' in which he tries to capture her. There is always something more to be said.

The poems of *The Green Helmet* (1910), the first volume in which Yeats tried out his new, abrasive style, explore a variety of responses to love. The first premise of them all is the suffering caused by Maud Gonne's disdainful independence, though he comes to terms with it in several ways. 'No Second Troy' and 'Reconciliation' both open with the idea of 'blame', only to shrink from following it through, the first by means of a rhetorical question that extends her destructive sway to revolutionary politics, seeing her as beyond control and self-control, a force of nature:

Why should I blame her that she filled my days
With misery, or that she would of late
Have taught to ignorant men most violent ways . . .?

It is difficult not to feel that Yeats is projecting onto the Dublin masses his own inability to make 'courage equal to desire'. Their baseness is contrasted with her 'mind / That nobleness made simple as a fire'. Her beauty unfits her for such a mundane world, being of 'a kind / That is not natural in an age like this'. This still, however, hints at the reproach that she is wasting her time on unworthy objects, and neglecting one who knows her real worth.

The poem, though a rhetorical *tour de force*, does not persuade us that its speaker has fully convinced himself. Made up entirely of a series of questions, the first two of five lines each and the last two of one line apiece, the poem's final effect is quizzical, not authoritative. When it asks 'Why, what could she have done, being what she is?' this does not simply testify to her being above all normal criteria of accountability. On the contrary it seems to invite all sorts of unspoken alternatives, though it answers itself only with another question: 'Was there another Troy for her to burn?' This somewhat caustically implies that the real motive behind her socialist agitations was not a desire for social justice but romantic craving to live in a more exciting, turbulent world than modern Dublin. It could be argued against Yeats that this was the primary motive behind *his* romantic nationalism.

The *femme fatale* may gain in grandeur from these mythical analogies, but she may also suffer by contrast, appearing no more than a spoilt upper-class adventurer, ready to sacrifice real if mediocre people on the altar of her passion. In 'Reconciliation', Yeats dodges blaming her only by projecting his accusations on to just these others. 'Some may have blamed you', he says, carefully dissociating himself from their petty carpings,

> that you took away
> The verses that could move them on the day
> When, the ears being deafened, the sight of the eyes blind
> With lightning, you went from me, and I could find
> Nothing to make a song about.

But all he will do is denounce that world, inviting her instead to cling close to him and share in 'our laughing, weeping fit'. This is hardly the mood in which to contemplate great political or poetic action. The possessive adjective 'our' carefully draws her in to a liaison with him which sets both against 'the world [that] lives as long ago', underwriting the final plaintive appeal, disguised as a statement: 'since you were gone, / My barren thoughts have chilled me to the bone'.

It is not a bad line in seduction, though. Both 'Reconciliation' and 'No Second Troy' are full of bad faith and evasion. But this does not detract from but rather enhances their *poetic* achievement, for they become poems in which the deceits and duplicities of love are honestly *enacted*, so that the poems reveal more than the speaker intends. It is as if, wearing the *mask* of the rejected lover, Yeats the poet says more about the role than he would consciously admit.

Indeed, this volume also contains that fine little lyric dialogue, 'The Mask', in which the woman asks him to remove his golden mask, so that she can know whether 'Love or deceit' lies behind it, and he refuses, unwilling to give away his true feelings, which, he insists, are irrelevant. It was the mask, he says, that engaged her mind and set her heart to beat, 'Not what's behind'. It is not the motive, but the act itself, which counts, he says. Wearing a symbolic mask, each can free him or her self from all that modern fretting about motive, aim and purpose, released into the joy of pure action. The act itself then becomes a mask in which energy and will are freed from explanation and recrimination. (In seventeenth-century theatre, a 'masque' was a drama of disguises in which all the characters wore masks.) As so often in Yeats, the metaphor for this is the fire that consumes itself:

> 'But lest you are my enemy,
> I must enquire.'
> 'O no, my dear, let all that be;
> What matter, so there is but fire
> In you, in me?'

It could be said that Yeats's attitude to this theme mellows as he gets older, but that would be only a half-truth. What in fact happens is that he begins to explore with greater subtlety the complexity of motive, conscious and unconscious, in any such relationship. In particular, he comes to consider the mixed motives on both sides that make for this complexity. The final stage in Yeats's handling of the theme is the acknowledgement of that truth (and truism) announced amidst a general list of losses in 'Nineteen Hundred and Nineteen':

> But is there any comfort to be found?
> Man is in love and loves what vanishes,
> What more is there to say?

The young lover's frustration and resentment flare up for a last time in the final lines of the latter poem. A poem which has been primarily about a world and a man 'lost amid the labyrinth that he has made / In art or politics' returns briefly to that more intimate labyrinth, speaking oddly and out of the blue, in a world full of violence, about a 'love-lorn Lady' bringing absurd presents to a 'stupid' and 'insolent fiend' that 'lurches past, his great eyes without thought'. The strange story is a veiled recall of Maud Gonne's infatuation with and marriage to the 'drunken, vainglorious lout' John MacBride. Yet it is so distanced, and so unexpected in the context, that it adds a final dislocation of perspectives to a poem which is all about expectations overthrown and hopes dashed.

From now on, Yeats's characteristic response to the theme of love is to bring it under the semblance of rule by transforming it into something else: a raging against and delight in transiency, a celebration of friends and friendship, a struggle with age and death, and an old man's positive re-evaluation of lust. In 'Beggar to Beggar Cried' in 1914 he had dramatically projected into the mouth of one beggar the intention to 'put off the world' and 'make my soul before my pate is bare', and into the mouth of the other the resolution to –

> '. . . get a comfortable wife and house
> To rid me of the devil in my shoes . . .
> And the worse devil that is between my thighs.'

In 'The Spur' in 1938 he summed up in own voice, with an aggressive, indignant rhetorical question, the mood of his last poems:

> You think it horrible that lust and rage
> Should dance attendance upon my old age;
> They were not such a plague when I was young;
> What else have I to spur me into song?

Like love, like his spirit voices, lust and rage had come to give Yeats metaphors for poetry.

3.15   AGE AND 'BODILY DECREPITUDE'

Yeats's whole volume *The Tower*, published when he was sixty-three, is preoccupied with age. 'Sailing to Byzantium', the opening poem, by way of preface turns its back on Ireland because it is 'no country for old men', and chooses instead the fabulous city of Byzantium with its 'Monuments of unageing intellect', its gold mosaics where ancient sages stand, freed from nature, 'in God's holy fire', finding in the realm of art 'the artifice of eternity'. The aged man is a mere scarecrow, 'A tattered coat upon a stick'. There is an inevitable clash between the failing body and the willing heart which, 'sick with desire', is 'fastened to a dying animal'.

In the major poems which follow this is a repeated motif. The title poem, which comes next, starts with an intemperate cursing at 'this absurdity . . . this caricature, / Decrepit age that has been tied to me / As to a dog's tail'. It goes on to contrast what it later calls 'the wreck of body, / Slow decay of blood, / testy delirium / Or dull decrepitude' with a mental and emotional energy which the failing body mocks:

> Never had I more
> Excited, passionate, fantastical
> Imagination, nor an ear and eye
> That more expected the impossible.

Denied the boy's physical capacity to match this mental exuberance, the poet fears that he must 'be content with argument and deal / In abstract things; or be derided by / A sort of battered kettle at the heel'. The desolation is such that, in section III of the poem, Yeats announces that 'It is time that I wrote my will'. In 'Meditations in Time of Civil War' he goes further, to fret over the possibility that his line may fall into decline, the inheritance be squandered by his successors, 'Through natural declension of the soul'.

The key exploration of this particular theme in *The Tower* is in the contrasted attitudes of the sequence 'A Man Young and Old'. This sequence is matched in the 1929 volume *The Winding Stair* by the sequence 'A Woman Young and Old', though Yeats had written it much earlier. It is in the idea of a beautiful woman's ageing, already touched on in 'Among School Children', 'In Memory of Eva Gore-Booth and Con Markiewicz' and other poems, that Yeats here explores the darkest aspects of the human condition.

Yeats wrote in 'After Long Silence':

> Bodily decrepitude is wisdom; young
> We loved each other and were ignorant.

Such ignorance has its own kind of wisdom, a 'carnal knowledge' superior to merely cerebral intelligence. It is in age that the force of such wisdom is most poignantly recalled, as in 'A Last Confession' from 'A Woman Young and Old':

> What lively lad most pleasured me
> Of all that with me lay?
> I answer that I gave my soul
> And loved in misery,
> But had great pleasure with a lad
> That I loved bodily.

She delights in recollecting the sheer animality of her sex. Her lover may have thought she gave him her soul when their bodies touched. But her real pleasure lay in knowing that 'Beast gave beast as much'.

'Her Vision in the Wood' (VIII in the sequence) carries such knowledge into a darker realm. Passion is inseparable from suffering, seizing the whole bodily frame in its obsessions. Now, 'Too old for a man's love' she stands 'Imagining men'. She thinks she can assuage the greater pang with a lesser one by masochistically tearing her body with her nails, drawing her blood so that 'its wine might cover/Whatever could recall the lip of lover'. What this summons up instead is a sadistic vision of a wounded man, carried in by mourning women like the dying Adonis, lover of the love goddess Aphrodite, gored in his sexual parts by a wild boar. She delights in his pain, as the dark, brooding sensuality of the last stanza makes clear, a *femme fatale* delighting in having her heart's torturer now in her power:

> That thing all blood and mire, that beast-torn wreck,

> Half turned and fixed a glazing eye in mine,
> And, though love's bitter-sweet had all come back,
> Those bodies from a picture or a coin
> Nor saw my body fall nor heard it shriek,
> Nor knew, drunken with singing as with wine,
> That they had brought no fabulous symbol there
> But my heart's victim and its torturer.

'Bitter-sweet' is almost too weak a fusion of opposites to describe this sado-masochistic relation, which Yeats seems to imply here is the deepest truth of bodily love. The sense of intoxication is most significant. This is almost an orgasmic fantasy of revenge. Her 'malediction', or curse, caught up in that 'contagion' of feeling, is the climax of a vision in which 'the dark changed to red' stirred by her self-laceration. The 'glazing eye' of the lover is one which merges sexual ecstasy with that of pain, and when her body falls and shrieks it is as if she is overwhelmed by passion, like the singers 'drunken with singing as with wine'.

Yeats has much to say on the theme of age. But it is in poems like these, where he explores the fury of the aged at the great gap between what they can imagine and what they can perform, that he penetrates to the darkest human recesses. It is this rage at bodily decrepitude and impotence that sets the mood for the ferocious apocalyptic vision of his last poems.

3.16 TERROR AND APOCALYPSE

There is for Yeats a wisdom that comes from beyond beauty, folly or madness – from terror itself. Yeats can at times seem an inordinately confident, assertive poet, assured of himself and of his convictions. Yet in a broadcast on Modern Poetry in 1936 he expressed what is perhaps his most abiding attitude – a profound scepticism about any certainties of belief:

> I think profound philosophy must come from terror. An abyss opens under our feet: inherited convictions, the presuppositions of our thoughts . . . drop into the abyss. Whether we will or no we must ask the ancient questions: Is there reality anywhere? (C, pp. 238–54)

The sequence of 'Supernatural Songs' which appeared in 1934 explores these ancient questions. The fictitious Ribh in 'Ribh considers Christian Love insufficient' has discovered that hatred can be a broom ('besom') to sweep the soul clean of its false convictions, so that 'From terror and deception freed it can/Discover impurities' and 'learn/A darker knowledge. . . .' This knowledge is one which dismisses intellectual roads to the truth, for 'Thought is a garment and the soul's a bride/That cannot in that trash and tinsel hide'.

In 'Whence had they come?', the eighth poem in the sequence, the carnal knowledge of love and sexual passion is also rejected as a means to true understanding. When young lovers awake from the passion they once proclaimed 'For ever and for ever', they do not even know what alien voices spoke through and possessed them. As if they were merely actors speaking an unknown author's lines, they are 'Ignorant what Dramatis Personae spake'. All deepest conviction is like this, the poem suggests. Even those who think in the marrow-bone are deceived. Yeats here espouses a radical scepticism which contradicts his own earlier utterances. He says of the aggressively active, outward-directed individual, 'A passion-driven exultant man sings out/Sentences that he has never thought'; while the inwardly-directed, masochistic Flagellant is likewise ignorant of 'what dramatist. . ./What master' dictates his suffering. In both cases, the individual is not the author of his acts or suffering, but merely the one through whom a deeper, impersonal meaning is expressed.

The poem then generalises this from the personal realm into an idea of history as itself the vehicle of meanings and purposes unknown to its actors. Human agents, pursuing ends of their own, may never know, or may discover too late, that what they intended to achieve is not actually what comes about. In retrospect, however, it often appears that the unintended outcome was an inevitable one.

The philosopher Hegel spoke of this as 'the cunning of reason', and saw the Emperor Napoleon as an instance. Apparently all-powerful, able to transform Europe by his military skills, Napoleon finally achieved a result totally contrary to his intentions, bringing about not France's but Britain's global predominance – something which, however, in the hindsight of history, seems a logical and even inevitable development.

Yeats's poem returns to a remoter history, speaking first of the barbarian invasions which destroyed the Roman Empire, and then the Emperor Charlemagne, the early French king, descended from those very barbarians, who first gathered the scattered fragments of Empire together again in the eighth century AD, and thus laid the foundations of modern Europe. Writing in 1934, Yeats clearly has in his mind that self-styled heir of Charlemagne and Napoleon who wished to reunite Europe by force, Adolf Hitler, who had come to power in Germany the previous year. Hitler for Yeats is the heir too of the barbarian hordes that had overwhelmed Roman civilisation. But that civilisation, grown decadent, needed to be overthrown in order to allow a new order to emerge. In 'A Bronze Head', Yeats expressed his belief that in the modern era only 'massacre' will save all that is worthwhile of 'this foul world in its decline and fall'. Here he writes of some of the agents of that salvation through destruction. This is what is known as an *apocalyptic* vision of history. In the New Testament, the 'Apocalypse' is that moment of total catastrophe in which the whole previous order of things is overthrown in a great cataclysm, preparing the way for the second coming of Christ. The word has subsequently been generalised to refer to any great cataclysm in which an old order of things is violently overthrown and replaced by something quite new. Thus Charlemagne's conception was a 'sacred drama' like the rape of Leda and the annunciation of Christ:

> Whence had they come,
> The hand and lash that beat down frigid Rome?
> What sacred drama through her body heaved
> When world-transforming Charlemagne was conceived?

It may be that in the present age Hitler, like his Fascist ally Mussolini in Itlay and his Bolshevik enemy Stalin, is one aspect of that 'rough beast', the Anti-Christ, that slouches towards Bethlehem to inaugurate a new and brutal era in the earlier poem 'The Second Coming'. Whatever the case, Yeats was convinced in the last years of his life, as he wrote in 1938 in 'Ireland after the Revolution', 'that some tragic crisis shall so alter Europe and all opinion' that a new order will come into being which harks back to 'the civilisation immediately behind that of Homer'. He looks forward enthusiastically, in an apocalyptic tone which recurs in these last years, to this new order. Once, he said, 'I still half-believed in progress', but no longer:

> civilisation rose to its high-tide mark in Greece, fell, rose again in the Renaissance but not to the same level. But we may, if we choose, not now or soon but at the next turn of the wheel, push ourselves up, being ourselves the tide, beyond that first mark. But no, these things are fated; we may be pushed up. (*C*, p. 271)

At the end of 'A General Introduction for my Work' in 1937 he had gone further, pouring scorn on the young English poets for their left-wing, progressive beliefs, expecting instead 'a counter-Renaissance' led by those 'strong enough to lead others' (which can only be a reference to the Fascist dictators), and rising almost to euphoria at its prospect:

> . . . but I go deeper than 'custom' for my convictions. When I stand upon O'Connell Bridge in the half-light and notice that discordant architecture, all those electric signs, where modern heterogeneity has taken physical form, a vague hatred comes up out of my own dark and I am certain that wherever in Europe there are minds strong enough to lead others the same vague hatred rises; in four or five or in less generations this hatred will have issued in violence and imposed some kind of rule of kindred. I cannot know the nature of that rule, for its opposite fills the light; all I can do to bring it nearer is to intensify my hatred. (*C*, p. 269)

It is out of such hatred and hope, the sinister delight in apocalypse and the consoling sense of a permanence that reasserts itself through total change, that the twelfth poem in the sequence, 'Meru', finds its motive force. Named after the sacred mountain at the centre of the Hindu paradise, the sonnet sums up Yeats's philosophy of history with a concision and clarity that makes *A Vision* almost redundant. Discussion of this poem is reserved for the Commentary section.

3.17   YEATS'S VISION OF HISTORY

Yeats's vision of history is set out in his book *A Vision*, first published in 1925 and reissued in a revised form in 1937.

As Yeats tells it in the Introduction (*C*, pp. 491–4), this book has a 'mystical' origin. After only four days of marriage, he says, his bride Georgie Hyde-Lees began to indulge in 'automatic writing' supposedly dictated by mysterious 'communicators' from the spirit world. These communications, shortly converted into spirit voices, Yeats was to work up into the elaborate pseudo-philosophical system set out in *A Vision*. This much rewritten book is in reality a fascinating and infuriating mish-mash of many traditional ideas, including much half-baked historical and metaphysical speculation and a great amount of intellectual garbage.

Yeats's spirits shrewdly informed him that their main purpose was to give him 'metaphors for poetry'. (A more self-critical man might have seen it as a reflection on the honeymoon.) They certainly fulfilled this function. In his apocalyptic poem of 1919, 'The Second Coming', Yeats speaks of his sight being troubled by 'a vast image out of *Spiritus Mundi*'. This '*Spiritus*' or '*Anima Mundi*' is, for Yeats, the repository from which all his most powerful symbols and images derive. Literally, it means the 'spirit' or 'mind of the world' spoken of in early mystical writings. In the notes to a poem he speaks of it as 'a general storehouse of images which have ceased to be a property of any personality or spirit'. In 'The Tower' he refers to 'images, in the Great Memory stored'. The work of the psychologist Carl Gustav Jung offered Yeats what he regarded as a 'scientific' explanation of it as the 'collective unconscious', that collection of archetypes we are supposedly born with – the race memory.

But the most powerful of Yeats's symbols, like the image of the Anti-Christ slouching towards Bethlehem in 'The Second Coming', do not need this backing to impress us. Rather it is the vigour of Yeats's language that gives us the frisson of terror, that sense of a supernatural force intensified here, for example, by the bestial as well as slovenly associations of the verb 'slouches'. The most important knowledge for understanding a poem such as 'The Second Coming' is a knowledge of contemporary history. The 'rough beast' of that poem is most centrally the beast of Bolshevism called up by the 1917 Russian Revolution, two years old when it was written, and engaged in a civil war backed by western military intervention. For Yeats, this was only the most potent instance of that 'mere anarchy' which was everywhere drowning the old imperial powers in a 'blood-dimmed tide', in the wake of the Great War. Ireland had seen the first revelation of this beast, at Easter 1916. A fanatical opponent of communist and 'mere anarchy', Yeats found himself in the anomalous position of supporting the violent men of the Irish liberation struggle, so that in other poems the 'rough beast' of 'The Second Coming' becomes naturalised as the heroic, supernatural figure of Cuchulain, summoned to Pearse's side in the ruins of a shell-torn Dublin.

3.18   THE GYRES

Many of the ideas of *A Vision* can distract from the poetry. They may even actually confuse the reading of a poem which is accessible without them. We do not, for example, *need* to know that the 'widening gyre' of the falcon's flight in 'The Second Coming' connects with his vision of history, and it could be argued that the connection actually diminishes the power and universality of the poem, making it a smaller, more thesis-ridden work than it is without this knowledge. Likewise, in 'Sailing to Byzantium' the phrase 'perne in a gyre' is perhaps the only major flaw in the poem, bringing in an extraneous and unnecessary complication to a poem otherwise transparent. (A 'perne' can be both a bobbin and a peregrine falcon; here, to complicate interpretation further, it could be either noun or verb.)

It is only in its large sweep that Yeats's philosophy is necessary to understand the poetry. In the poem, 'The Gyres', for example, we need to know only its barest outlines. The title invokes his most notorious concept (usually pronounced with a hard 'g'). The poem can be very simply paraphrased: an old man, facing death, takes a kind of heady consolation from the fact that all things pass and come around again, and delights in charting the details of the modern disintegration. Even thought itself, we're told, gets worn out. Beauty and worth outlive themselves; 'ancient lineaments' (the lines of a face, with the hint perhaps of a family lineage preserved by family features) suffer extinction.

The present age (the late 1930s), the poem suggests, is a time of such extinction on a large scale. The blood-dimmed tide of 'The Second Coming' has been released on the earth. By a kind of transference, the ancient Greek philosopher Empedocles (who believed all things are a mingling of the four elements, held together by love or separated by strife, perpetually entering into new configurations) is held responsible for the present disorderliness in things. Another Troy is about to burn, like all those old civilisations put to the sword in 'Lapis Lazuli'. But 'what does it matter?' Yeats asks. All that we need to do is '"Rejoice!"' This poem is a powerful expression of Yeats's delight in an apocalyptic view of things.

'Old Rocky Face' in 'The Gyres' represents that supernatural world beyond history, from which, in Yeats's mysticism, all true meanings derive. In 'The Man and the Echo' it becomes 'Rocky Voice'. This poem however implies that the supernatural voice of the oracle is only the echo of human explanations, projected onto the abyss and coming back to us as divine wisdom. Yet significantly, though the Voice reiterates the man's words with the instructions 'Lie down and die' and 'Into the night', it does not echo as a command the last word of his argumentative and unanswered question: 'Shall we in that great night rejoice?'

By contrast, 'The Gyres' suggests that the only attitude to take towards all this tumult is to 'laugh in tragic joy', accept and rejoice in whatever is coming, and stand above it. This is the posture taken by the Hamlet and Lear of 'Lapis Lazuli', who embrace 'Tragedy wrought to its uttermost' with a 'Gaiety transfiguring all that dread'. For, as Yeats says there:

> All things fall and are built again,
> And those that build them again are gay.

The recurrence of all things links these poems with the poem Yeats chose to make the vehicle of his own epitaph, 'Under Ben Bulben'. Here again he tells us, speaking of the eternal return, that 'Gyres run on'. In 'The Gyres' recurrence is enacted by the way in which the word 'gyres' returns at the end, having been exclaimed twice at the very beginning of the poem, confirming stylistically what it claims as a truth, that 'all things [will] run / On that unfashionable gyre again'. But what are these 'gyres'?

In *A Vision* Yeats conceived of history as composed of two cones, rotating in opposite directions, the apex of each at the centre of the other's widest arc, as in the diagram on p. 108. Every moment in time moves through these opposing spirals. Any one moment thus contains two antithetical, interpenetrating movements, for one cone is widening as the other, whirling in the opposite direction, narrows. These spiralling motions are the gyres. The times of maximum historical turbulence are those where the gyres reverse their motions. These great historical reversals occur every cycle of two thousand years (the 'Great Year'), at those moments where the previously expanding cone begins to contract and the previously contracting cone to expand.

Throughout history, the interpenetration of the gyres means that one dominant historical principle, the primary phase, is always shadowed by its antithesis, the objective by the subjective, and vice versa. The rape of Leda by a god in the shape of a swan is thus reversed in the annunciation of the dove to Mary. Christ, as the male god of love, reverses the female bringer of strife, Helen. In turn, these phases of the Great Year are reproduced in the twenty-eight 'Phases of the Moon', set out in Yeats's poem of that name, and explained at length in *A Vision*.

Before the full moon of history, the subjective principle holds sway, and men seek fulfilment in themselves, in mastery of thought and action. After the full, men turn outwards, towards the objective world, before which they shrink in servitude, as in our own era. But the complete darkness without any moon of the twenty-eighth phase, that of complete objectivity, brings a reversal, a movement back to subjectivity. It is in the movement between these antithetical gyres that human history and personal life are shaped.

In some of the later poems, a knowledge of the philosophy certainly helps to elucidate what is otherwise obscure in poems which get a great deal of their power from the esoteric doctrine they propound. But most of Yeats's poetry can be approached without worrying too much about this doctrine. For those who are interested in the philosophy, however, the clearest exposition and analysis is probably that of Northrop Frye, in *An Honoured Guest* (see Guide to Further Reading, section 3). A note to the volume *Michael Robartes and the Dancer* offers the following explanation and diagram.

The figure . . . is frequently drawn as a double cone, the narrow end of each cone being in the centre of the broad end of the other.

It had its origin from a straight line which represents, now time, now emotion, now subjective life, and a plane at right angles to this line which represents, now space, now intellect, now objective life; while it is marked out by two gyres which represent the conflict, as it were, of plane and line, by two movements, which circle about a centre because a movement outward on the plane is checked by and in turn checks a movement onward upon the line; & the circling is always narrowing or spreading, because one movement or other is always the stronger. In other words, the human soul is always moving outward into the objective world or inward into itself; & this movement is double because the human soul would not be conscious were it not suspended between contraries, the greater the contrast the more intense the consciousness. The man, in whom the movement inward is stronger than the movement outward, the man who sees all reflected within himself, the subjective man, reaches the narrow end of a gyre at death, for death is always, they contend, even when it seems the result of accident, preceded by an intensification of the subjective life; and has a moment of revelation immediately after death, a revelation which they describe as his being carried into the presence of all his dead kindred, a moment whose objectivity is exactly equal to the subjectivity of death. The objective man on the other hand, whose gyre moves outward, receives at this moment the revelation, not of himself seen from within, for that is impossible to objective man, but of himself as if he were somebody else. This figure is true also of history, for the end of an age, which always receives the revelation of the character of the next age, is represented by the coming of one gyre to its place of greatest expansion and of the other to that of its greatest contraction. At the present moment the life gyre is sweeping outward, unlike that before the birth of Christ which was narrowing, and has almost reached its greatest expansion. The revelation which approaches will however take its character from the contrary movement of the interior gyre. All our scientific, democratic, fact-accumulating heterogeneous civilization belongs to the outward gyre and prepares not the continuance of itself but the revelation as in a lightning flash, though in a flash that will not strike only in one place, and will for a time be constantly repeated, of the civilization that must slowly take its place. This is too simple a statement, for much detail is possible.

3.19 APOLLONIAN AND DIONYSIAN

In the work of the nineteenth-century German philosopher Friedrich Nietzsche Yeats found a *dialectical* vision of history that appealed to his imagination. Yeats took delight in dialectic, that is, the clash of opposites, believing that every synthesis was something produced by fierce conflict between a thesis and its antithesis. In particular, Yeats found useful a key opposition in Nietzsche's *Birth of Tragedy* (1872) between two contradictory impulses. In a letter in 1903 he wrote:

I have always felt that the soul has two movements primarily: one to transcend forms, and the other to create forms. Nietzsche calls these the Dionysiac and the Apollonic respectively.

These two modes can be seen to correspond to the antithetical gyres of *A Vision*. The word 'form' links ideas about order in art with ideas about order in society. The Dionysian principle, named after the Greek god of wine and orgiastic frenzy, is an anarchic energy simultaneously destructive and creative, instinctual, passional, derived from the unconscious, the blood, the race memory. The Apollonian, named after the god of order, poetry, reason, eloquence, is the principle of conscious control, the articulating, shaping and informing principle. In art, it turns the raw materials of experience into beautiful, harmonious forms, giving them rebirth as an idea, something intended, complete. In society, it brings the chaos of human passions under a semblance of rule.

At some moments (for Nietzsche and Yeats at the high point of Greek society in the fifth century BC, and for Yeats in early Byzantium) these forces can enter into perfect equilibrium for a brief period. When they do, they produce great art which is the synthesis of mighty opposites (see C, pp. 495–504). Then, inevitably, one or other of the elements becomes predominant, unity dissolves, and a decadence sets in, in which either too much energy or too much formal order leads to a falling away from harmony. As one force grows in power, the other declines, until an extreme is reached, and then the antithetical force stages a comeback and begins to wax as the other wanes.

In A Vision and in 'The Phases of the Moon', Yeats sees this larger millenial waxing and waning reflected in the twenty-eight phases of the lunar cycle, in which each night corresponds to a stage of history, the period up to the full of the moon being that of physical action and adventure, the period after that of passivity and flight, and the full moon itself the point at which, briefly, body and mind are united and, 'Under the frenzy of the fourteenth moon, / The soul begins to tremble into stillness'. For Yeats these are the moments of great historical reversal, such as were brought about, for example, by the births of Helen of Troy and Christ and, in our own era, are prefigured by the upheavals of world war and revolution.

In a time of great social and political turbulence like that of Yeats's own age, such a simple philosophy seemed to explain a great many contemporary events. A Vision makes it clear that he saw his own age as one moving towards such a catastrophic reversal. 'A civilisation', he wrote there, 'is a struggle to keep self-control', and 'the last surrender, the irrational cry, revelation', is announced by 'the scream of Juno's peacock'. It is this that we hear announcing the end of Ascendancy graciousness at the close of the third section of 'Meditations in Time of Civil War',

heralding the coming desolation of section IV and the violence
and turmoil of civil war that is to appear in sections V–VII.

3.20   REPETITION, SHADOW, ARCHETYPE

In a note to the poem 'An Image from a Past Life', Yeats suggests
that those images which, in dream or reverie, seem to float up
from the *Spiritus Mundi*, are really visitations from a past life:

> Those whose past passions are unatoned seldom love living
> man or woman but only those loved long ago [in an earlier
> life], of whom the living man or woman is but a brief symbol
> forgotten when some phase of some atonement is finished.

The face that 'becomes to the living man an obsession, continually
perplexing and frustrating natural instinct' may be one that
recalls someone loved incompletely in an earlier life, of whom
the present beloved is a copy or manifestation, and it may be
'only after full atonement or expiation, perhaps after many lives,
that a natural deep satisfying love becomes possible'.

Behind this is Yeats's idea, derived from Neo-Platonic thought,
that in the world of history all things are only shadows of the
original *paradigms*, *types* or *archetypes* which exist eternally. They
have fallen away from this original perfection down the levels
of time in the way that water spills over from basin to basin of
the fountain at the beginning of 'Meditations'. Thus the modern
poet in that poem is a mere shadow of Homer, and Maud Gonne
is simply a repetition of Helen of Troy, with whom, 'The Tower'
tells us, 'the tragedy began'.

The difficult and allusive 'Two Songs from a Play' reveals
Yeats's sense of history as a drama in which each individual
event is a re-enactment and transformation of some earlier event.
In the play *Resurrection* from which the songs are taken, the
annunciation, crucifixion and resurrection of Christ rerun but
also transform the fate, in Greek myth, of Dionysus. The 'fierce
virgin', Christ's mother Mary, then repeats, and combines, the
roles of the 'staring virgin' Athene, who rescued Dionysus'
heart, and of Semele, on whom Dionysus is begotten for a
second time by Zeus in the form of a lightning flash. The image

which closes the second poem ('What ever flames upon the night/Man's own resinous heart has fed'), reproduces the lightning flash as the star of Bethlehem followed by the three wise men, or 'Magi' (magicians).

In the poem called 'The Magi' Yeats speaks of the wise men of the Nativity story as 'pale unsatisfied ones', still waiting for some revelation that will go beyond the Christian one, creating a 'turbulence' in the gyres of history greater than that caused by Calvary, by releasing 'The uncontrollable mystery on the bestial floor'. So here, in the second song, the 'Galilean turbulence' which Christ brings into the world inaugurates an era of 'fabulous, formless darkness'. The 'Odour of blood' of the crucifixion puts an end to the rational philosophy and art of Greece, replacing both 'tolerance' and 'discipline' (not antitheses but mutually sustaining and complementary principles) by their brutal parodies – 'mere anarchy' (as in 'The Second Coming') and authoritarian violence.

In the long perspectives of history, nothing endures for ever. Yet in a sense the pattern, the Platonic 'Idea', 'type' or 'archetype' endures, and is endlessly repeated. The 'Magnus Annus' referred to in the first stanza is the 'Great Year' of Platonic philosophy described in Book IV of *A Vision* – that enormous period of time during which ' "the whole of the constellations shall return to the positions from which they once set forth, thus after a long interval re-making the first map of the heavens" ' (pp. 245–6). Within this vast circling of time there are lesser cycles, Yeats suggests, such as the phases of sun and moon. But

> It is impossible that any single form . . . should come into being which is exactly like a second, if they originate at different points and at times differently situated; the forms change at every moment in each hour of the revolution of that celestial circuit . . . thus the type persists unchanged but generates at successive moments copies of itself as numerous and different as the revolutions of the sphere of heaven. (p. 253)

Events and individuals are thus different 'forms' of the same unchanging 'type'. In the final vibrant image of the poem, 'man' is self-consuming, self-devouring, all his actions in turn devoted to achieving that completion which will also bring them to an end. The heart torn out of Dionysus' side and then reborn as a new Dionysus becomes a heart that feeds the self-consuming fires of history.

But of course, if each historical event is merely a repeat of some earlier, primal one, it loses part of its reality, and the sacred drama can very easily come to appear merely 'a play', something which need not be taken seriously because all the suffering in it is illusory. Thus the first song can envisage a repetition of Troy's 'rise and set'. The phrase sufficiently resembles, and is sufficiently different from, the cliché 'decline and fall of the Roman Empire' to hint at what this second Troy is as well as how it differs from the first. It is that Roman Empire which stood appalled before the 'fabulous darkness', because what it faced in Christ was its own destruction, repeating that of Troy. We cannot fully understand Yeats's idea of history without considering the enormous importance to it of this theme.

3.21 TROY, LEDA, HELEN, ADAM

Troy provides one of the most recurrent themes in Yeats's poetry. The excavations of Heinrich Schliemann at Hissarlik in Turkey had demonstrated to Yeats's generation a whole new historical dimension to what had previously been thought of as myth. Troy had become the symbol of a superior civilisation destroyed by barbarians – the warring Greek princes under Agamemnon, who, Yeats tells us in *A Vision*, 'broke up a great Empire and established in its stead an intellectual anarchy'. In Yeats's thought, Troy's fall stands at a turning point in the gyres of history, at which a new annunciation occurred. The precise moment of this turning point is the conception of Helen of Troy herself, the product of a divine intervention in history like that which later produced Christ, and now, in the modern era, has given birth after two more millennia to the Anti-Christ of 'The Second Coming'. In Book V of *A Vision*, 'Dove or Swan', Yeats observes that 'I imagine the annunciation that founded Greece as made to Leda . . . and that from one of her eggs came Love and from the other War'. The sonnet 'Leda and the Swan' focuses on that moment of annunciation.

Yeats's sonnet, unlike its sources, presents the rape from the point of view of the woman, the victim. The distress of Leda is emphasised by the double question which takes up the whole of the second quatrain, where the verb 'push' and the noun 'rush' stress the intense brutality of the rape in contrast with the weakness and terror of 'those terrified vague fingers'. Note how physically precise is that Anglo-Saxon noun 'shudder' contrasted with the latinate and abstract verb 'engenders': Leda is reduced from 'girl' to mere 'body', the physical means by which terror enters history. The frightened, helpless questions are not only Leda's but ours also. We share in her anxiety and distress, for we too are involved in this moment of violation. Our history issues from it, for Love and War are generated here.

Helen is not even mentioned here, for she is merely the vehicle for this 'first multitudinous revelation' – the burning of Troy, the death of Agamemnon, and all that follows from them. The moment of impregnation is also the moment at which the god withdraws from Leda and from history, a closure indicated by the abrupt way in which the polysyllabic 'Agamemnon' is brought up 'dead' halfway through a line. Women, whether Leda or Helen, seem unimportant here, except as vehicles of patriarchal power and the agencies of male death (Agamemnon was murdered by his wife). Both mother and child are 'mastered', a favourite word of Yeats's, by this power which is simultaneously more and less than human, divine and 'brute' at once. His will accomplished, Zeus is 'indifferent' to the woman, lets her drop. She, however, has been 'caught up' (which works a significant change on the first 'caught' in line 3), so that in the end she has taken on some of the divine ferocity which her child comes to impose upon men.

Agamemnon's death and the deaths of all those male heroes at Troy can thus be seen as fitting punishments for the brutality imposed upon the female. Leda – it is kept as a question to ensure our continued unsureness and insecurity – may have put on Zeus's knowledge as well as his power. But this is simply the knowledge that all things pass away, that the act (of coition as well as war) consumes and extinguishes itself as it is consummated.

In 'Among School Children', Maud Gonne is herself linked
with Helen as a 'daughter of the swan'. A sequence of short
early poems had already made the connection. 'No Second Troy'
sees her socialist agitations as part of the same historical
destructiveness. She has 'taught to ignorant men most violent
ways, / Or hurled the little streets upon the great'; and he asks:
'Why what could she have done, being what she is? / Was there
another Troy for her to burn?' In one of his earliest poems, 'The
Rose of the World', he had first announced this theme, again of
Maud Gonne:

> Who dreamed that beauty passes like a dream?
> For these red lips, with all their mournful pride,
> Mournful that no new wonder may betide,
> Troy passed away in one high funeral gleam,
> And Usna's children died.

The archetype of 'this lonely face' outlives and underlies the
changing catastrophes of history, is in fact the motive force for
all its tragedies and wonders. By contrast, 'men's souls . . .
waver and give place', ephemeral servants of that which they
think they have mastered.

The second stanza of 'Long-Legged Fly' provides the link
between Troy and Rome which we have already seen hinted at
in 'Two Songs from a Play'. This is the poem in full:

> That civilisation may not sink,
> Its great battle lost,
> Quiet the dog, tether the pony
> To a distant post;
> Our master Caesar is in the tent
> Where the maps are spread,
> His eyes fixed upon nothing,
> A hand under his head.
> *Like a long-legged fly upon the stream*
> *His mind moves upon silence.*
>
> That the topless towers be burnt
> And men recall that face,
> Move most gently if move you must

> In this lonely place.
> She thinks, part woman, three parts a child,
> That nobody looks; her feet
> Practise a tinker shuffle
> Picked up on a street.
> *Like a long-legged fly upon the stream*
> *Her mind moves upon silence.*
>
> That girls at puberty may find
> The first Adam in their thought,
> Shut the door of the Pope's chapel,
> Keep those children out.
> There on that scaffolding reclines
> Michael Angelo.
> With no more sound than the mice make
> His hand moves to and fro.
> *Like a long-legged fly upon the stream*
> *His mind moves upon silence.*

In the first stanza Yeats refers to the political and military leader of imperial Rome, Caesar. In the last he refers to the artist of Catholic and Renaissance Rome, Michael Angelo. In the second stanza, he alludes without naming her to Helen of Troy, by echoing a famous line from Christopher Marlowe's play *Dr Faustus*: 'Was this the face that launched a thousand ships, / And burnt the topless towers of Ilium?' The link is a buried one.

Helen fell in love with the son of the King of Troy (Ilium), who abducted her thither, bringing about the ten year siege which ended in the burning of that city. For the Latin poet Virgil, writing his *Aeneid* in praise of Augustus Caesar, Helen was thus indirectly responsible for the foundation of Rome, since if Troy had not been destroyed the Trojan hero Aeneas would not have fled from its burning ruins to Italy, where his descendants were said to have established a new Troy in Rome. Helen in Yeats's poem thus becomes the unnamed connection between Caesar's and Michael Angelo's Rome, and Rome becomes the archetype of the eternally renewed city.

For Yeats such figures as Helen, Caesar and Michael Angelo are archetypes of the kind we have already considered – figures of a recurrent pattern in human experience and history, representing the will to power of the soldier/emperor, the will to passion of the beautiful woman, and the will to create of the artist. The most noticeable feature of this poem is the refrain, which links together these three figures, generalising what they have in common yet, it seems, curiously unrelated to each.

The three figures are themselves very different: Caesar stands for military power, empire, rule, order, strategy, planning, the Apollonian principle, extending and consolidating an empire by war. Helen stands for that 'terrible beauty' which can destroy a civilisation. Michael Angelo, the painter, represents art, whose images of both love and war transform them, turning suffering into a celebration of civilisation. Each individual, however, penetrates beneath the surface of things, to the eternal archetypes. Their minds are not simply the conscious selves that tread the delicate, tensioned surface of the water. They are also the deeper silence of the stream itself – the unconscious or *Anima Mundi*. The mind contemplates that silence as the fly floats upon the stream. Each of these three individuals represents in some sense a figure of apparently careless mastery.

Helen is an image of beauty so powerful it can drive men to destroy civilisation. Her sexual energy is both destructive and generative. Compared with the aristocratic Caesar, she is a street-wise urchin, not the traditional semi-divine queen, but someone who 'practise[s] a tinker shuffle'. She is an amateur still learning, and learning from the wrong sources. If Caesar is the looker, his eyes fixed on nothing, she is looked-at, though she 'thinks . . . That nobody looks'. She will always be looked-at: this is her fate. Helen's anarchic beauty touches the quick of history, for without her there would have been no Caesar or Michael Angelo. The masterful mind of war and art derives its power from the subversive flesh of Helen, the female life-giving and life-removing power.

In the final stanza, Helen's successors, 'girls at puberty', are as reckless and indifferent as she, caught up in the intrigues of the flesh. Yet, just as Caesar's order involves violence, so Helen's disorderliness involves order. A 'tinker shuffle' may not be much of a dance, but it is nevertheless related to that image of the dancer merging with the dance we have encountered in 'Among School Children' and other poems. When practice has made perfect, we will not be able to tell the dancer from the dance here also.

The final stanza provides a synthesis of these opposing forces. It shifts from creative war and destructive passion to an art which reconciles them. Nietzsche argued that, in great tragic art such as the drama of Sophocles or Shakespeare, the Apollonian principle of order and the Dionysian principle of energy are reconciled in a perfect, creative harmony. In the magnificent images of Michael Angelo's paintings on the roof of the Sistine chapel (in a Rome which is the centre of a spiritual, not a secular empire), the real is transformed into the ideal through the mastery of the artist's skill.

The restlessness of adolescence may equally be transformed if the female imagination can grasp the appropriate image of male perfection on which to focus and define its feelings. As so often, this poem of Yeats's turns out to be partly about education, about the education of the emotions, and about art's role in achieving this. It calls up a poem such as 'Among School Children', and explains why Helen figures there too. Michael Angelo's Adam embodies a universal ideal in a particular image. He is 'the first Adam' in several senses: the first man, from whom all other Adams are descended, the Platonic paradigm of maleness. And he is also the foremost image of the male on which girls should fix their growing thoughts. Michael Angelo depicts what his fellow Florentine Dante also sought, according to Yeats in 'A People's Theatre' (1919): 'His study was Unity of Being, the subordination of all parts to the whole as in a perfectly proportioned human body.'

There can be no Helen of Troy, no female principle, without a corresponding male principle. These antithetical images to our own selves are revealed to us through personal love, but also in the great archetypes of history and myth. The masterful images of art, whether Michael Angelo's Adam or Homer's Helen, offer the most perfect and lucid representation of the archetypes which shape our imagination. In a Preface to his *Poems* (1899–1905) Yeats wrote that 'All art is in the last analysis an endeavour to condense as out of the flying vapour of the world an image of human perfection'. As he was to write in 'A General Introduction for My Work', in such images 'nature has grown intelligible and by so doing a part of our creative power'.

3.22 DEATH AND REBIRTH

Yeats's idea of the archetypes is closely bound up with the contemplation of death. In *The Winding Stair* this theme becomes more urgent but also more considered than in the earlier poetry. In 'Death', the poet distinguishes between animal and human experiences of death. The animal, without self-consciousness, is unaware of death in advance, simply dies; but 'A man / Awaits his end / Dreading and hoping all' because, possessing the ability to envisage the future, 'Man has created death'. Nevertheless, this means also that he has overcome it, can cast 'derision upon / Supersession of breath'. By seeing death as the mere discontinuance of a physical process, Yeats seems here to downgrade its importance.

We die many times before our death, Yeats thinks. Every defeat, but also every victory in which 'A great man in his pride / Confront[s] murderous men', is part of this rehearsal for death. What we see in this volume is no longer the anxiety of *The Tower* but a new calm in confronting supersession. In 'A Dialogue of Self and Soul' Soul advises Self to 'Fix every wandering thought upon / That quarter where all thought is done', i.e. death. In the second part of the poem Self declares that it is 'content to live it all again / And yet again', to face up to death and rebirth. The little deaths in which the soul is mortified (including the 'folly' of love) are also entry into richness, into the 'most fecund ditch' of life. Love, that is, is a series of deaths and rebirths prefiguring the greater death.

At times, Yeats seems actually to believe in the transmigration of the soul – the idea that at death or some time thereafter it is reborn in another body, returning to live out the same pattern of fate in another circle of the gyre. In 'The Cold Heaven' we see the perplexity of that soul at the moment of being cast out. In the 'Byzantium' poems and elsewhere the living man is reborn as a work of art. In other poems, such as 'The Delphic Oracle upon Plotinus' or 'Cuchulain Comforted' this is changed to rebirth in some Neo-Platonic or Celtic underworld. Yeats's ideas were not consistent on the question of survival after death. What is central to all of them, however, is the idea of preparing oneself with dignity and graciousness for that instant of transit.

What Yeats is doing in these poems is announced in 'Vacillation'. The foliage of Lethe (the river of death and forgetfulness in Greek mythology) can be renounced in this life by one who, in the Irish idiom, begins to 'make his soul', that is, prepare for death by testing all acts and decisions against that thought. Death and life are again related to 'breath', here extravagantly wasted if not directed towards the highest achievement possible in defiance of death:

> No longer in Lethean foliage caught
> Begin the preparation for your death
> And from the fortieth winter by that thought
> Test every work of intellect or faith,
> And everything that your own hands have wrought,
> And call those works extravagance of breath
> That are not suited for such men as come
> Proud, open-eyed and laughing to the tomb.

Pride and laughter, as in 'Dialogue', become the prerogatives of one who has rejected 'The trivial days' and their preoccupations. It is this which allows the self to enter into a happiness that can bless and be blessed. Or, as 'Dialogue' says, measuring the lot, forgiving oneself the lot, frees one momentarily from fear:

> When such as I cast out remorse
> So great a sweetness flows into the breast
> We must laugh and we must sing,
> We are blest by everything,
> Everything we look upon is blest.

'At Algeciras' is subtitled 'A Meditation on Death', and the calm of that word 'meditation' indicates the new access of tranquillity which has come to the poet in facing up to personal death. It is a remarkable poem in its understatement, its low-key lines and its concession to the inextricable mixture of squalor and glory in a world where the beautiful birds 'feed on some foul parasite'. The birds cross the straits of Gibraltar to Morocco to light 'In the rich midnight of the garden trees' as the poet's own soul must cross the river of death to enter, perhaps, equally rich surroundings.

At sixty-three, the ageing Yeats, as so often in these later poems, reverts to memories of boyhood to define his existence in the here and now. Looking across the straits of death is first cast in homely and reassuring terms before expanding into the grandeur of intellectual enquiry. As a boy he often carried home for an older friend's pleasure 'actual shells of Rosses' level shore'. The levelness of that shore in its modesty becomes, like the relative ignorance of the boy, a metaphor of the soul's ignorance faced by the vast waters of death. But death is also something he wishes to enquire into in the way that Sir Isaac Newton, the founder of the modern era by his discoveries in physics, enquired into the nature of the universe. At the same time, Newton acknowledged humbly that 'to myself I seem to have been only like a boy, playing on the seashore, and diverting myself, in now and then finding another pebble or prettier shell than ordinary, while the great ocean of truth lay all undiscovered before me'.

Humility is deepened in the final stanza. Though now Yeats's imagination is bid to run 'much on the Great Questioner', it is death, in the end, which will ask questions of the dying man, and not the other way round. Even here, though, pride is reconciled with humility in that quietly 'fitting confidence' in which a soul prepared for death can face these questions with dignity and restraint. Restraint is indeed the hallmark of this fine poem. And, with its sense of an ending, leaving unresolved whether death ends life or is merely the prelude to some greater adventure, it is an appropriate poem on which to end this exploration of Yeats's themes.

4

Style

Yeats was perhaps the twentieth century's finest stylist. At the end of his essay 'William Blake' he quotes his great predecessor's remarks on style:

> 'I have heard people say, "Give me the ideas; it is no matter what words you put them into"; and others say, "Give me the design; it is no matter for the execution" . . . Ideas cannot be given but in their minutely appropriate words, nor can a design be made without its minutely appropriate execution.' (C, p. 32)

This is Yeats's position too. For him, poetry is 'the natural words in the natural order'; and this goes all the way down to the most 'minutely appropriate' level. Even punctuation is part of a poem's form.

A frequently used concept in modern criticism is that of *foregrounding*. By using a specific device to call attention to a word or group of words, the poet places it in the foreground of our attention, as, in a painting, figures or objects in the foreground will be the first to catch our eye. Any literary device can be used to foreground certain words or ideas.

Even the positioning of a punctuation mark can make a considerable difference to a poem's pace and impact. In 'An Irish Airman Foresees his Death', the comma between the two nouns in the line 'Nor law, nor duty bade me fight' is not strictly necessary, but together with the somewhat literary construction (instead of 'Neither law nor duty') it makes us pause to think about the contrast Yeats is suggesting, between externally imposed 'law' and internally dictated 'duty'. It maks us see too how the two aspects of this antithesis parallel the two in the succeeding line, 'Nor public men, nor cheering crowds'. Public men *impose* law; cheering crowds *elicit* duty.

As a poet whose imagination works *dialectically*, through the conflict and resolution of opposites, Yeats is naturally drawn to the stylistic device of *antithesis* revealed here – the formal balancing of one word or phrase against another. Here it reinforces the idea that Gregory has himself 'balanced all, brought all to mind', and weighed 'In balance with this life, this death'. Antitheses of this kind are frequent in Yeats's verse. The device can sometimes be found in a highly compact form, as for example, where *oxymoron* joins contradictory ideas or images as adjective and noun. The most famous instance of this is perhaps the phrase 'a terrible beauty' in 'Easter 1916'. The 'murderous innocence of the sea' in 'A Prayer for My Daughter' is another. At times, the contrast between two ideas can be so extreme as to seem a *paradox*, that is, an impossible yoking of opposites, as in the noun and verb 'ice burned' in 'The Cold Heaven'. This kind of literary paradox was common in Renaissance poetry and is often known as a 'Renaissance conceit'.

Metre is often used as a way of foregrounding an idea. Most English poetry is based on some variation of the regular *iambic* metre, in which an unstressed syllable is succeeded by a stressed one. But it is the variation which is important. Since Shakespeare, the most familiar of English metres has been the *iambic pentameter*, five iambics in a row, whether unrhymed, as *blank verse*, or rhymed as *heroic couplet* or in some more complicated stanza form.

Yeats is a master of the pentameter, but his mastery arises from his ability to set up a musical contrast and interplay between the *metrical norm* and the ordinary rhythms of speech. This is sometimes called *counterpoint*. In a poem such as 'The Gyres' below, the opening line announces the metrical norm as iambic pentameter. But already, in the last foot of the line, the regular sequence of unstressed/stressed syllables is disrupted by the feeling that the word 'look' has some kind of stress, even if it is not quite as heavy as that on 'forth'. This uncertainty is confirmed by the next line, where the first foot is clearly two heavy stresses, and the light weak stresses around the middle of the line likewise depart from the iambic norm. By the time we come to the third and fourth lines, we are ready, even relieved, to have that norm reaffirmed, in lines which are perfectly regular metrically. A *counterpoint* has been set up between our awareness of the norm and the poet's departures from it, and this contributes much to our pleasure in the sound of the poem. It also serves to focus our attention on the idea at the centre of these lines:

> The Gyres! the gyres! Old Rocky Face, look forth;
> Things thought too long can be no longer thought,
> For beauty dies of beauty, worth of worth,
> And ancient lineaments are blotted out.

Poets frequently use emphatic sound patterns for similar effect. Foremost among these is *alliteration*, the repetition of initial or medial consonants. Here the repeated 'th' sound calls our attention to the idea of things and thinking, and the relation between them. Again, note the way the repeated 'n', 'm' and 't' in the following line from the same poem reach a particular concentration in the key words 'numb nightmare', where 'm/n' and 't/m' come uncomfortably together. The difficulty of pronouncing the phrase clearly, together with the heavy stress, then combine with the alliteration to foreground these key words:

What *matt*er though *numb n*ight*m*are ride *on t*op.

Another such device is that of *assonance*, the repetition and play upon the same or similar vowel sounds ('night' and 'ride' above). Often this involves interweaving long and short vowels. Note how the long open vowels of the following line from 'Under the Moon' come to an abrupt stop at the line ending with the short vowel 'sun', only to begin again with an even more complex interweaving of alliteration and assonance in the next line:

Land-under-Wave, where out of the moon's light and the sun's
Seven old sisters wind the threads of the long-lived ones.

In the poem 'In Memory of Eva Gore-Booth and Con Markie-wicz' discussed below, the open vowels of 'evening', 'light', 'Great', 'open' give the effect of a quiet clarity and fullness of being, and render all the more abrupt the transition from the memories of youth and beauty to the violent 'raving' and 'shears' with which they are destroyed. This makes 'autumn', unlike evening, a time not of graceful decline but of brutal violation, and associates summer with the dignified pathos of a 'wreath' suddenly ravaged by time. Sound and sense are difficult to dissociate here.

Sometimes the echo of a word's rhythm can have a similar effect. In these lines from 'The Municipal Gallery Revisited' it is impossible to say how much of the poignancy comes from the echo, almost a rhythmic rhyme, of 'Heart-smitten' and 'emotion':

> Heart-smitten with emotion I sink down,
> My heart recovering with covered eyes;
> Wherever I had looked I had looked upon
> My permanent or impermanent images.

The effect here is reinforced by another familiar device of Yeats's – the *repetition* of a word or phrase, often with a variation upon its meaning. This is particularly rich in the present instance, not only in the repetition of 'looked' and 'permanent' but in the *paranomasia* or *play on words* of 'recovering' and 'covered'. In the four lines from 'The Gyres' above there is a similarly complicated interweaving of repeated words.

An extreme form of paronomasia is the *pun*. This does not have to be funny. 'The Cold Heaven' has at its centre a pun which defines the whole emotional turmoil of the poem. The poem's opening word ('Suddenly') signals by its own suddenness the dazzling, desolating shock of the insight the poem records. As readers we are plunged into the middle of things, sharing with the poet in the traumatic nature of his revelation. We are not told what this revelation is. Rather we have to experience the bewilderment for ourselves before we can understand it.

The apparently downbeat middle line, 'And I took all the blame out of all sense and reason', expresses the central emotional *ambiguity* of the poem. Does it mean that senselessly, *against* all reason, he finds himself taking all the blame for his failure in 'love crossed long ago'? Or does it mean that now, shocked 'out of all sense and reason' by his sudden insight, he realises for the first time that he *should* take all the blame? As readers, we share in this conflict of interpretations, and a key pun focuses the conflict for us.

He is, we are told, 'Riddled with light'. This is true in a punning double sense. The light, the insight he has just had, riddles him like bullets. But it also presents him with an unanswerable riddle. This riddle is focused in the concluding question of the poem, which links his perplexity with that of a ghost, freed from the 'Confusion of the death-bed' only to confront the 'injustice of the skies for punishment'. 'Injustice' implies his innocence. 'Punishment', however, implies the opposite, acknowledged guilt. Being riddled with the light of one revelation only exposes him, and us as interpreters of his experience, to a new riddle. The pun foregrounds the crisis of interpretation which the poem presents. This crisis can be resolved only by paradox as, in a further pun, the ghost at death is said to begin to 'quicken' (i.e. come alive as well as speed up).

The usual feature of such shocks is the certainty of the revelation they afford. But here Yeats manages to put over a sense of shocking certainty in a poem which remains disturbingly equivocal. The richness of the poem derives from this very refusal to answer the questions for us; we too are left dramatically unsure of what we have witnessed.

Yeats tried to hammer his thoughts into a unity by the rhetorical power of his *syntax*, the order and construction of his sentences. Again and again we read poems in which a single sentence drives through a whole stanza, pausing at line ending for dramatic effect, or sweeping magisterially on, articulating and organising all its many images and ideas under the rule of one dominating thought. Yeats's is a characteristically 'masterful' syntax in this way. His syntax seems to assert his power and authority over what he says, over the images and ideas he uses, even when he is writing of defeat and despair.

The opening stanza of 'Meditations in Time of Civil War' illustrates how syntax interacts with stanza form. The syntax here performs two major functions, forcing upon us the logic of an argument announced by the opening 'Surely' while at the same time enacting the exuberance of the water it describes:

> Surely among a rich man's flowering lawns,
> Amid the rustle of his planted hills,

Life overflows without ambitious pains;
And rains down life until the basin spills,
And mounts more dizzy high the more it rains
As though to choose whatever shape it wills
And never stoop to a mechanical
Or servile shape, at others' beck and call.

The phrases introduced by 'among' and 'amid' set the leisurely scene by delaying the main thrust of the sentence, which when it does come in line 3 seems itself to overflow without the effortful ambition of which it speaks. Then the semi-colon slows down the syntax, in further enactment of this leisureliness, leading into the two clauses in apposition introduced by 'And'. Here life rains down itself, spills slowly over the line ending only to mount again at the beginning of the line. The repeated 'more' repeats too the raining down at the next line ending, dizzying us with all this unending movement. This is a sentence which now, we note, moves on without any retarding punctuation. By this time the sentence has passed its high point, and the subordinate clause beginning 'As' endows this with a studiedly casual feel, as if to emphasise the choosing and the willing. And then, as if in final enactment, the sentence itself begins to stoop towards its conclusion, diminishing the 'mechanical' shape by placing it as an unsatisfactory, almost muttered rhyme. At the same time the repeated 'shape' in its vagueness tells us how unimportant this declining section of the sentence is, even in its dismissal of 'others' beck and call'. Yet placing this phrase at the end, on a closing rhyme, adds a discordantly subversive note to the effortless activity so far described. This is confirmed by the next stanza, for before we can sink content into this aristocratic ease and mastery, we are pulled up abruptly by a line which begins with the abrupt, repeated dismissal of it all as 'Mere dreams, mere dreams!'

Another major device of Yeats's which is illustrated here is the use of *half-rhymes* of various kinds, to give a dissonant or disturbing effect to a poem. 'Lawns' and 'rains', for example, are *slant rhymes*, with only the 'ns' sound linking the two words. There is also an instance of an *offbeat rhyme* – rhyming a stressed with an unstressed or lightly stressed syllable. Only the pull of a regular pentameter makes the barely stressed '-cal' of 'mechanical' rhyme with 'call'. The fact that each syllable begins with 'c' adds insult to injury, for if this were a full rhyme it would, ironically, be no rhyme at all, since you cannot rhyme a sound with itself.

Instances of such half-rhymes abound in Yeats, and can be found in almost every poem. A similar effect can be seen in the rhyme of 'distress', where the second syllable is heavily stressed, with the weakly stressed 'clumsiness' in the passage from 'A Dialogue of Self and Soul' discussed below. The particular effect achieved will depend on the overall context. In 'Under Ben Bulben', for example, the rhyme of 'up' and 'top' interacts with the *inversion* of the phrase 'top to toe' to reinforce the sense of shapelessness of which it speaks:

> Scorn the sort now growing up
> All out of shape from toe to top . . .

In 'The Circus Animals' Desertion', 'in vain' in the first line rhymes with 'broken man' in the third, to give a sense of this vanity and brokenness, but the effect is then modified by the full rhyme in line 5 with 'began', though the sense of uncertainty is continued by the rough couplet which concludes the first stanza: 'Those stilted boys, that burnished chariot, / Lion and woman and the Lord knows what.' Like the Lord, however, Yeats knows exactly what he is doing here, communicating to us just that mixture of exasperation and disappointment, qualified by a deeper conviction of achievement, which is the theme of the poem.

Yeats's stylistic virtuosity is highly self-conscious. In 1926 he wrote to Herbert Grierson, in whose edition of the poems of John Donne he had found a model for his style, that 'My own verse has more and more adopted . . . the syntax and vocabulary of common personal speech'. A 'natural momentum in the syntax', he went on, is 'far more important than simplicity of vocabulary', and enables a poem to carry 'any amount of elaborate English'. In 1937 he spelt this out in 'A General Introduction for My Work':

It was a long time before I had made a language to my liking;

I began to make it when I discovered some twenty years ago that I must seek, not as Wordsworth thought, words in common use, but a powerful and passionate syntax, and a complete coincidence between period and stanza. Because I need a passionate syntax for passionate subject-matter I compel myself to accept those traditional metres that have developed with the language. (*C*, pp. 265–6)

This 'complete coincidence between period [sentence] and stanza' is a characteristic feature of his work. Even when he is using a rigorous form, however, the characteristic Yeatsian effect is achieved through deliberate departures from the norm. Yeats uses a wide variety of *stanzas* with consummate skill, often deploying highly elaborate rhyming schemes. One of his most powerful effects, however, is achieved in stanza V of 'The Municipal Gallery Revisited' by suddenly and as if arbitrarily dropping a whole line from the stanza form he has established, leaving us with a sense of distress at unfulfilment similar to that the poet feels.

More often, though, there is a complete coincidence, as in the passage from 'Meditations' above, between period and stanza. Much of his effect is obtained by the way in which he alternates different kinds of sentences and clauses within a stanza, and plays them against the stanza form. Frequently he will foreground a key word by placing it at the beginning or end of a line (the latter doubly emphasised by being a rhyming position). Often he combines this with *enjambement*, the sentence running over the line ending instead of pausing at it. The last two lines of 'After Long Silence' set up a tension in our expectations in this way, since on the one hand 'young' seems to require us to run on, and yet the half-hidden antitheses between age and youth and wisdom and ignorance make us poise on this pivotal word. Certainly, it is quite unusual to have a single word isolated at the line ending after a major pause of the kind indicated by the semi-colon:

> Bodily decrepitude is wisdom; young
> We loved each other and were ignorant.

In the following stanza from 'A Dialogue of Self and Soul'

enjambement focuses our attention on the word 'distress'. But this is more effective because it comes after three sentences each of which is *end-stopped* – confined within a single line – and of which two have a similar, repeated structure. Though the two questions seem to be completed, they are in fact carried over into the long trailing clause which begins with 'Endure', which does not make sense unless it is seen to be in apposition to 'live it all once more', taking 'What matter if I . . . once more' as its understood precondition. The listing of verbless noun phrases then mimes the incompleteness of which it speaks, each phase of growing-up isolated from every other. The effect is compounded by the enjambement on 'pain', while the superficially unsatisfactory rhyme on 'clumsiness' seems an enactment of its sense:

> A living man is blind and drinks his drop.
> What matter if the ditches are impure?
> What matter if I live it all once more?
> Endure that toil of growing up;
> The ignominy of boyhood; the distress
> Of boyhood changing into man;
> The unfinished man and his pain
> Brought face to face with his own clumsiness;
>
> The finished man among his enemies?

Not only do we have to wait for the sentence to be finished at the beginning of the next stanza, but we have to wait till then to discover that this sentence is cast in the form of a question, taking up and amplifying the questions that opened the stanza, and leading on to the questions that follow.

Yeats is such a virtuoso that he can even cut short his own elaborately developing sentence across a line and stanza ending, as in 'The Tower':

> Hanrahan rose in frenzy there
> And followed up those baying creatures towards –
>
> O towards I have forgotten what – enough!

Placing a clause or clauses in a way which interrupts or delays the natural flow of a sentence can add dramatic tension to a situation. In 'After Long Silence', for example, the short main clause 'it is right' is followed by three lines of qualifying clauses which set the scene *in which* it is right, before we come to *what* is right ('That we descant and yet again descant/Upon the supreme theme of Art and Song'). In a different vein, Yeats can use crisp short statements in which a sentence or a clause is confined to one or two lines in order to give an authoritative, axiomatic quality to what he is saying, as in the second of 'Two Songs from a Play'.

Inversion of the normal word order of a sentence can have a peculiarly dramatic effect. In 'Byzantium', placing the verb 'flit' at the end of a line, before rather than after the noun which is its subject ('Flames') calls attention to both words, an effect reinforced by alliteration and enjambement. This suggests the weird, out-of-place quality of the fire and the flitting. The adverbial phrases of time and place ('At midnight on . . .'), likewise out of their natural sequence, emphasise the supernatural reordering of the ordinary, daily world, while also arousing our expectation that something strange is going to be revealed. This strangeness is then compounded by the *negative* constructions in which the flames are defined. We can see how much of the effect is derived from the word order by rearranging the sentence into a more conventional form:

> At midnight on the Emperor's pavement flit
> Flames that no faggot feeds, nor steel has lit,
> Nor storm disturbs, flames begotten of flame . . .

(Flames flit on the Emperor's pavement at midnight. No faggot feeds, no steel has lit and no storm disturbs these flames, which are begotten of flame.)

For all his skill at producing complex stanzas with elaborate rhyme schemes, a great number of Yeats's poems are in the popular measure of the *ballad*, usually in some variation of the quatrain, rhyming *abcb*, made up of lines which alternate four and three stresses. In 'The Pilgrim' he restores the ballad measure to its original Elizabethan form as 'fourteeners' (fourteen syllables with seven stresses to a line, rhyming as couplets), and adds a nonsense *refrain* common in the ballad form. This reinforces the sense of a mind with its 'wits astray' from fasting and devotion as once from drinking and sex.

Yeats often extends the ballad form by complicating the metric pattern, introducing many dramatically irregular lines, with extra stresses or syllables, doubling the quatrain, or adding a repeated refrain of one or two lines. Such popular forms do much to undermine many high-falutin' attitudes, as in the 'Crazy Jane' poems, with their attacks on establishment cant and hypocrisy in the name of the proud body.

'Mad as the Mist and Snow', with its heavy, songlike stresses and emphatic rhyme (the third repetition of which always brings in the refrain announced in the title) is one such poem. It subverts all intellectual pretensions – whether Horace, Homer, Plato, Tully or Cicero – in the name of the hapless flesh, using a mock *demotic* language: 'How many years ago/Were you and I unlettered lads/*Mad as the mist and snow?*') to stress that underneath all the fine thought there is the same madness, lust and rage against the 'foul winds' of life. The refrain implies that we are all equally out in the mist and snow.

'I am of Ireland' is a variation upon an Irish fourteenth-century dance song which supplies the opening, middle and closing stanzas of the poem. But its complex rhythms and the doubled quatrain form of its two original stanzas (rhyming ababcdcd with several near-rhymes) build up to make a disturbing commentary on the popular song. It is a cryptic and menacingly incomplete narrative, in which 'One solitary man/Of all that rambled there' responds to the words of a song, but whose response remains unclear except for its vehemence.

The refrain in 'Long-Legged Fly' works in a similar way, as does that in 'The Wild Old Wicked Man'. Here the abrupt and apparently unconnected, unrhymed refrain '*Daybreak and a candle end*' interrupts a racy dialogue between old man and young woman with what seems like an authorial reminder that time passes and candles burn down; but it also allows for the idea of burning the candle at both ends and other, more ribald possibilities.

Yeats's use of the refrain in this *disjunctive* relation to the stanza implicates the reader in the text. We have to supply some of the connections Yeats has left out or implied. Many of his best poems work like this, by leaving a great deal unsaid, leaving us to read between the lines and interpret the juxtaposition according to our own desires, fears or anxieties. The refrain thus introduces a mysteriously oracular and sonorous note into the proceedings, leaving us unsure what the connection is between main text and refrain, but convinced that something deeply meaningful is being said.

A poem can use its grammatical forms in very complex ways. In the poem 'In Memory of Eva Gore-Booth and Con Markiewicz' mentioned above I pointed out how assonance can work to register the different attitudes towards time and its passage in the poem. But the poem also uses the very *tense* of its verbs to similar effect. Before the mood of the opening lines takes hold, for example, it is dispersed in the shift to a larger, wearing sense of time as something dragged out, extended too long:

> The light of evening, Lissadell,
> Great windows open to the south,
> Two girls in silk kimonos, both
> Beautiful, one a gazelle.
> But a raving autumn shears
> Blossom from the summer's wreath;
> The older is condemned to death,
> Pardoned, drags out lonely years
> Conspiring among the ignorant.
> I know not what the younger dreams –
> Some vague Utopia – and she seems,
> When withered old and skeleton-gaunt,
> An image of such politics.
> Many a time I think to seek
> One or the other out and speak
> Of that old Georgian mansion, mix
> Pictures of the mind, recall
> That table and the talk of youth,
> Two girls in silk kimonos, both
> Beautiful, one a gazelle.

This shifting in and out, compacting action into a brief spurt and then varying into a long-drawn-out momentum is the key to the poem's play with the idea of time. Time, it suggests, is subjective (the second paragraph of the poem affirms this). The absence of a main verb from the opening sentence allows the poet to place the scene he describes in a timeless intermediate realm where it is neither memory nor presence, but comes alive as if born anew in the poem.

The verb 'shears', in the present tense, turns an act which happened once for each individual into a recurrent process happening perpetually to someone. The continuation of this present tense to describe acts and experiences now clearly terminated by death has a peculiar effect, for it summons up dead scenes and people as if they were still alive (as, in his recollections, they still are). The point he is making is that friendship reclaims the dead, keeps them alive. Thus he can go on to say not 'Many a time I thought to seek [them] out' but 'I think to', carrying the thinking on into a future in which it may yet happen.

'Recall' likewise becomes not the summoning up of a dead past, but its recreation, projected into a future which has not yet happened. In this way the return to the description of the girls in silk kimonos projects what is in fact a memory into a prospect, in an eternal return that transcends ordinary linear time. This leads on to the apparently direct address to the dead women in the last lines of the poem, calling them up both as they *are* ('shadows') and as they *were* in the remote past, 'both / Beautiful, one a gazelle', while omitting the intermediate time of separation in which they became 'withered old and skeleton-gaunt'.

In this way the women remain forever 'The innocent and the beautiful', and can be addressed, called on to do something, in the here and now. Note the circularity of this: he bids them to bid him to strike a match, and then he will bid them to run (which he is already bidding them to do now, as if time had already caught fire). The great gazebo of time is built by human beings (an architectural folly but also a place to gaze from) and can be burnt down by them. The last line in its command is also an appeal: tell me you still live by bidding me to burn down time and thus ensure that you live. The poem is its own gazebo, building the trans-temporal eternity of friendship of which it speaks. The dramatic effect is achieved by the way in which the very grammar, the tenses of the verb, burn down the ordinary logic of time.

Yeats often sounds self-assured, even arrogant, in his pronouncements. Often, this is the assumption of a mask within the poem itself. ('The Mask', already discussed, explores the psychology of such a practice.) If we look closely at his poetry, we see that this arrogant assurance everywhere dissolves into uncertainty, hesitation, anxiety, that there is a different person beneath the mask. Yeats is in fact the great master of *ambivalence*, of the *equivocal* in feeling and thought. This is not only a matter of mixed feelings. It is also a case of one mood slowly undermining or rapidly overwhelming another, of sudden changes of tack in argument and feeling, swift or gradual reversals of tone and assumption.

One way this is revealed is in the *dramatic* manner in which he approaches a subject. By this I do not refer primarily to his experiments with verse drama, though these clearly had an effect on his poetry. Rather it is the sense of his poems as little *psycho-dramas*, which in a short space *enact* shifts of mood and awareness, often exploring contradictory attitudes, without committing themselves to any one in particular, much as a playwright remains aloof from the conflicting points of view of his characters.

Often, these contradictory points of view are presented through dialogue, as in 'A Dialogue of Self and Soul', 'Ego Dominus Tuus' and the 'Crazy Jane' and 'Michael Robartes' poems, or 'The Mask' itself. Frequently, while dividing his text between two voices, he will also provide a *framing narrative* in his own voice, or at least in the voice of an assumed *authorial persona* (the character or mask he has assumed in order to narrate the poem). Examples of this are 'The Phases of the Moon' and 'Solomon and the Witch'. Sometimes it seems to be the reader, or the person addressed, who is the silent second party to a dialogue, as in 'Politics', 'The Spur', 'The Curse of Cromwell'. Frequently, too, the drama is all within the one psyche, as if the one mind were in active, argumentative dialogue with itself. Such poems are usually known as *dramatic monologues*, in which the poet, either in his own voice or assuming that of a *persona* (or 'mask') speaks out his inmost thoughts and feelings in all their complexity and contradictoriness, and we seem to be overhearing him rather in the way we overhear a Shakespeare soliloquy.

Take, for example, 'Friends', a poem in which Yeats sets out to celebrate three women who have had an effect on his life, only one of whom is Maude Gonne. The opening line ('Now must I these three praise') almost seems to announce the poem as a deliberate exercise in which he will maintain a balanced and even tone. It is as if he were setting himself the task of writing about Maud in a context which minimises her disturbing power. This is certainly the case at the beginning, as he speaks first of Olivia Shakespear (a long-term friend with whom he had an affair in 1896). Here he says, very positively, that with her no thought or care 'Could ever come between/Mind and delighted mind'.

With Lady Gregory too the tone is all positive, and he speaks of her encouragement and understanding which 'So changed me that I live/Labouring in ecstasy'. But the tone shifts a little with the uncertain questioning which introduces Maud Gonne, as if the poet for the first time realised the difficulty of the task he had announced in the opening line. 'And what of her that took/All till my youth was gone/With scarce a pitying look?' he asks, and then, tersely, 'How could I praise that one?'

The answer comes dramatically, not from thought but from feeling, welling up physically, overwhelming the mere cerebral weighing of pros and cons. The poem too is overwhelmed dramatically in the process, turning from being an equable celebration of friends to an impassioned testimony to the power of love, which flows through it, transcending and as it were minimising the mere 'delight' and 'ecstasy' associated with the other two women. The poem too is shaken from head to foot:

> When day begins to break
> I count my good and bad,
> Being wakeful for her sake,
> Remembering what she had,
> What eagle look still shows,
> While up from my heart's root
> So great a sweetness flows
> I shake from head to foot.

Like many of Yeats's poems 'Friends' derives its emotional ambiguity from what we may call its *subtext*. This is the tale that lurks beneath the poem's conscious story, like the subtitles to a foreign film, but perhaps telling a totally different story, revealing what critics have called *the unconscious of the text*. This *textual unconscious* can be read out from the imagery of the poem, its sudden changes of tack, its shying away from certain matters, or the way in which ideas not part of its conscious argument keep returning to plague the speaker. The recurrence of a particular *motif*, that is, a repeated image or idea, can alert us to this subtext. This is particularly apparent in long poems, which allow for a certain *discursiveness* or wide-ranging quality to their narrative. Some of Yeats's most powerful dramatic monologues fall into this category.

'The Tower', for example, is a *meditative* or *reflective poem* which seems on the surface to be preoccupied with the poet's fretting over approaching death and what he will leave behind him. Yet throughout the text, the motif of irrational and unrequited love struggles to raise its head, and is repeatedly *repressed*. This is part of the drama of the poem, setting up a contrary current in section II, for example, which expands from the excessive devotion of the serving-man to Mrs French, through the drunkards 'maddened' by the beauty of a peasant girl glorified by a song, into full flowering as the image of Helen of Troy, who 'has all living hearts betrayed'.

Yeats does not here make a direct connection with his own personal experience, not even hinting at the woman he usually linked with Helen. An underground current, however, leads on to the fictional character Hanrahan of whom Yeats had written twenty years before. Just as he is about to retell this story, as we have seen, Yeats breaks off dramatically, interrupting his own narrative with a curt 'enough!', changing the subject in mid-sentence from Hanrahan's 'horrible splendour of desire' to someone completely different – a man not even love, music or revenge could cheer. Yeats claims to have forgotten what happened to Hanrahan. But in fact, he has repressed the memory because it is still painful. *Interruption* of this kind is a powerful device in narrative.

But he cannot keep it repressed. It surfaces once more as he returns to think of Hanrahan, an 'Old lecher with a love on every wind'. Hanrahan, he says, has already, confronting a death like that which Yeats now faces, 'Reckoned up every unforeknown, unseeing / Plunge, lured by a softening eye, / Or by a touch or a sigh, / Into the labyrinth of another's being'.

Lost in similar labyrinths, still unclear what happened to him over Maud Gonne, Yeats finally comes clean on what is obsessing him in this poem, something which arises from that 'troubled heart' whose urgings he had tried to control in the opening lines. Once again, it is only as a question that he can countenance it; and, furthermore, as a question to a dead (and fictional) character of his own invention, who is therefore unlikely to answer. The question, however, seems to answer itself as it is asked, and the dramatic tension of the poem is expressed in the doubleness with which the question implies its answer, revealing the poet's own divided feelings. The stanza invites us to assess a range of interpretations of his past acts, balancing self-criticism and self-justification. We note in particular the shift from 'cowardice' to 'conscience'. While unsure of his motives, it is clear about the effects of his choice:

> Does the imagination dwell the most
> Upon a woman won or woman lost?
> If on the lost, admit you turned aside
> From a great labyrinth out of pride,
> Cowardice, some silly over-subtle thought
> Or anything called conscience once;
> And that if memory recur, the sun's
> Under eclipse and the day blotted out.

Then, dramatically, this revelation too is blotted out, in a further act of repression, and the section ends and a new one begins on a totally different tack: 'It is time that I wrote my will'.

Yeats's poetry is full of such *rhetorical questions* – questions used for dramatic effect, almost as exclamatory devices, without expecting an answer. The rhetorical question often becomes a way of introducing into the text an element that could not be contemplated directly, as in the passage just cited from 'The Tower'. He may use it to permit an intrusion from the realm of the fantastic, the mythical or supernatural which would not have been possible in a straight statement. By asking a question, Yeats establishes the reality of that which he wishes to assert, before we can reject it. In 'The Second Coming' it is the rhetorical

question which first introduces the idea of a supernatural
revelation:

> Surely some revelation is at hand;
> Surely the Second Coming is at hand.

In 'To Dorothy Wellesley' he goes further, supplying an answer
to his curt question 'What climbs the stair?' straight out of Greek
myth. Though he only defines this negatively to begin with, his
negative rapidly changes into full-bodied detail:

> Nothing that common women ponder on . . .
> The proud Furies each with her torch on high.

In Shakespeare's *Henry IV, Part 1*, in reply to another piece of
Celtic blarney – Owen Glendower's claim to be able to call spirits
from the vasty deep – the bluff Hotspur replies, 'Why, so can I
. . . But will they come when you do call for them?' Yeats allows
us no room to make such a sceptical response. His rhetorical
questions, one might say, beg the question.

One of the features of Yeats's style which gives it a decidedly
dramatic and immediate quality is his deployment of what
linguistic philosophers call *performative utterance*, that is, a statement which *performs* the very act it refers to ('I name this ship'
said in the very moment of naming). Consider, for example,
how, in 'Easter 1916', Yeats gives a peculiar immediacy to his
celebration of the executed men by proclaiming 'I write it out in
a verse'. Here he closes the distance between him, them and
us – writer, written about and reader – by linking us all in a
single act which collapses time into a perpetual present tense in
which all share. The writing is here and now; we are supposedly
there with Yeats at the very moment of writing, just as he wishes
to impress us with how close he feels to the murdered men.
The performative sentence in fact enacts what he is claiming for
their action – that it is a deed which has taken them out of time,
the mere succession of history, into some eternal realm in which
a true Ireland now will always exist:

> Now and in time to be,
> Wherever green is worn,

> Are changed, changed utterly:
> A terrible beauty is born.

It is worth asking whether the final line is itself not a performative statement, in that it gives birth to the very thing it claims, just as simply by speaking of them Yeats *invents* Cuchulain stalking through the Post Office, the Furies climbing the stairs, and the rough beast slouching towards Bethlehem to be born. The question of the performative, that is, leads directly into Yeats's idea of art's power to *create* reality, to invent a world which then becomes part of our imaginative being – the power, in the words of 'The Tower', to 'Dream and so create / Translunar paradise'. And indeed, this very statement of Yeats's aesthetic begins with a clearly performative act, the announcement that:

> I mock Plotinus' thought
> And cry in Plato's teeth,
> Death and life were not
> Till man made up the whole,
> Made lock, stock and barrel
> Out of his bitter soul.

The mocking is uttered in the very act of proclaiming that he mocks, just as, at the beginning of this section of the poem, a declaration of intent, in the future tense, becomes the *performance* of that intent, in the present: 'It is time that I wrote my will' becoming the writing of which it speaks. In the context of each of these utterances, Yeats is attempting to enact in his very sentence structure, his use of tense, for example, the compacting or collapsing of time of which he writes.

Mockery and gibing are common in Yeats's Ireland. But his response is a more haughty *irony*, the aristocrat's tone of contempt. When, because of its sometimes contradictory associations, an image or motif points to more than one meaning, there is clearly the possibility of irony in a poem. In irony what is said contains another meaning from that on the surface. This other meaning may be heard by one person (perhaps only the speaker) but not by another, and this alternative meaning subverts the surface one. (Hotspur's reply to Glendower above is ironic, in that it picks out an ambiguity in Glendower's boast, the double meaning of 'call', and turns it back on the user.)

An instance of irony deliberately intended and part of the content of the poem is Yeats's memory, in 'Beautiful Lofty Things' of his father's carefully timed punch-line, rebuking the audience of the Abbey Theatre: '"This Land of Saints", and then as the applause died out, / "Of plaster Saints"; his beautiful mischievous head thrown back'. Here the irony is contained in the first phrase, since the speaker knows what is coming next and the audience does not. The audience expects to be flattered and instead finds itself insulted. The discrepant awareness, between what it expects and he intends, is then resolved by the punch-line, which pulls the mat from under the audience's feet.

Irony can run through a whole poem (see, for an example, the discussion of 'Michael Robartes and the Dancer' in Chapter 3.11). At its crudest, this is revealed in the sarcasm of 'September 1913', which clearly does not endorse the venal attitudes it seems to posit, as the refrain to each stanza makes clear. It can be revealed in a casual aside, as in 'To a Shade', which imagines Parnell's ghost looking at his monument and then in parenthesis adds the damning afterthought '(I wonder if the builder has been paid)'. Dubliners are no better at paying their financial debts than their debts of honour. More generally, it can pervade a poem as a kind of subversive tone, indicated by image and allusion, as in the strange and scarifying 'High Talk', with its apparently self-dismissive but in fact angry and indignant assertion, 'Malachi Stilt-Jack am I, whatever I learned has run wild / . . . All metaphor, Malachi, stilts and all'. Yeats is a master of *tone*, and irony, one of the most difficult literary phenomena to pin down, runs through many of his finest poems, at times indicated by a mere twitch of style, a raised eyebrow of nuance, at times by a thunder of disapproval.

Yeats's *diction* is always distinctive. His range of vocabulary is wide. There are a great many words of sensual and sensory experience, with a decidedly physical, *tactile* or *kinetic* quality to them. He prefers words which have a very specific, concrete impact. Cuchulain 'stalked' through the Post Office. In 'Cuchulain Comforted', his soul 'strode among the dead', he did not merely 'walk', and the dead 'muttered' and 'Came creeping up', rather than simply 'speaking' and 'approaching'. Yeats's poetry is particularly full of this bodily or *corporeal* language. Just as his syntax is dynamic and energetic in its movement, so his vocabulary is full of verbs of motion and activity. This emphasis is there in his preoccupation with the idea of the dancer, as well as in his decidedly physical love poetry, and for Yeats emotions such as hatred, anger, fear are themselves felt 'in the marrow-bone'. If he is afraid, in 'Presences', 'it seemed / As if the hair stood up on my head'. Age in 'The Tower' is not simply an abstract state but 'has been tied to me / As to a dog's tail'.

Yet for all its physicality of detail this opening passage from 'The Tower' contains three other words to describe age, 'absurdity', 'caricature', 'decrepit', which point to another aspect of his diction. Yeats not only writes of the body, he also writes extensively of the mind, the imagination, the soul. But he rarely thinks of them as disembodied things. Rather, the mind for Yeats is the body thinking, and the imagination moves with all the vigour and turbulence of the flesh. In a song from one of the plays, he refers to 'His mind that is fire, / His body that is sun', and goes on to speak of being 'Preyed upon, fed upon / By jealousy and desire', deliberately using metaphors rather than similes based on 'like'. This attitude is reflected particularly clearly in his vocabulary. One of his characteristic tricks is to insert a sudden *polysyllabic* word, usually *latinate* in origin, into a sentence otherwise comprised largely of shorter words of Anglo-Saxon provenance. ('Polysyllabic' is itself one such word, a word of several syllables, in this case derived from Greek.)

Such words are usually thought to be more abstract and unemotional than the ordinary run of English diction, but Yeats often reverses this expectation. In 'September 1913' the third stanza begins with a highly visual image, the flight of the wild geese, in a sentence which is almost entirely made up of Anglo-Saxon words of one syllable, and a somewhat prosy list of names. But then the sentence closes with a startlingly original idiom, 'All that delirium of the brave'. The normally clinical word 'delirium' takes on a precise and powerful significance as a description of the folly and grandeur of the lost heroic tradition of 'Romantic Ireland'. In 'Long-Legged Fly' the word 'puberty', an even more clinical and unpoetic word, like 'civilisation' at the beginning of the poem, adds vigour and contrast to the verbal mood, linking Helen of Troy practising a tinker shuffle with the teenage girls in the Pope's chapel. 'A Bronze Head' has many instances of such swift shifts of verbal *register* (level of diction), juxtaposing two polysyllables with two near clichés, for example, and making something completely new out of their interplay, in the lines 'Propinquity had brought/Imagination to that pitch where it casts out/All that is not itself'. Yeats is surpassed perhaps only by Shakespeare in his ability to plumb the metaphoric possibilities of the latinate word, in a poem such as 'A Prayer for my Daughter' ranging from 'heart-revealing intimacy', through birds 'dispensing round/Their magnanimities of sound', to 'her opinionated mind', before homing in on the 'accustomed, ceremonious' vocabulary of the final stanza, in which custom and ceremony are celebrated.

Yeats's early poetic diction lacked this vitality, being full of mist and vapidities, in an idiom which was over-literary and over-refined. The great achievement of his later poetry is to recover the vocabulary and idioms of everyday speech, the *colloquial* and *demotic* tones of the spoken word, while combining this with an intellectually rich and varied range of reference. Yeats's language can be coarse and racy, vulgar and refined, or it can be sharp, acerbic and rancorous, but it is rarely dull.

A poet's *vocabulary* is always personal, and the critic can usually distinguish the work of one poet from another by the kind of words he or she uses. Poets have favourite words, but they may also be notable for the range and variety of the words they use, the kind of areas from which they derive their vocabulary – for example, from religion, or science, or philosophy, or from everyday life. Now, with the aid of the computer, it is possible to make a more scientific, consistent assessment of a poet's vocabulary. Such a study reveals not only the frequency with which certain words are used, but also the diversity of a poet's vocabulary. Yeats's vocabulary is extremely wide, and is drawn from a wide variety of sources. Altogether, he uses over 10,000 different words in his poetry. The average person can make do with two to three thousand words of active vocabulary, and 5000 words is unusually rich for ordinary conversation.

Yeats's vocabulary also changes considerably between early and late poetry. In 1942 the American poet Randall Jarrell, in an essay called 'The Development of Yeats's Sense of Reality' (*Southern Review*, 7, 1942) compiled comparative lists of some of the commonest words in Yeats's early and late poetry. The contrast between the two vocabularies is significant. Jarrell himself commented that in the early poetry: 'The metre and construction match the words; the limp wan rhythms, the enormous quantities of adjectives and intransitive verbs, are exactly what one would expect'; whereas in the later poetry: 'The words are full of violence, of toughness and strength; some have a rhetorical magnificence, others a sensual colloquial sharpness. This list is the antithesis of the other; one needs only to read the two to realise how completely Yeats's poetry changed'. The following are the words he picked out in early and later verse:

> Dream, rose, heart, lonely, wandering, gentle, sorrow, sweet, mournful, holy, tender, quiet, faery, Druid, beauty, peace, lofty, high, pitiful, wan, murmur, worn, grief, tears, weary, sigh, old, desolate, piteous, faint, dreaming, foam, flame, fade, woven, tremble, shadowy, grey, dim, white, pale (curd-pale, cloud-pale, honey-pale, pearl-pale, death-pale).

> Foul, passionate, ignorant, ignorance, malicious, abstract, crazy, lunatic, mad, bitter, famous, frenzy, frenzied, violent, violence, fantasy, rage, daemonic, horrible, furious, bloody, triumphant, insolent, arrogant, arrogance, mock, mockery, murderous, bone, blood, stone, malice, sensual, fanatic, intellect, shriek, rascal, knave, rogue, fool, gyres, miraculous, cold, indifferent, raddled, blind, wild, naked, dumb, rag, ragged, tumult, joy, death, hate, night, wine, ditch, mummy, barren, murderous, torn, terrible, great, brilliant, fabulous, drunken, mire.

A great deal can be learnt about a poet's work by examining his most frequently used vocabulary. Since Jarrell's time, the critic and student of Yeats have benefited from having available a statistically accurate checklist of the poet's vocabulary. This is *A Concordance to the Poems of W. B. Yeats* (1963), edited by Stephen Maxfield Parrish. The book lists all the words Yeats uses, citing each line and poem in which they occur. Thus we can see at a glance not only what words the poet most likes to use, but where he uses them, and what other words they consort with. We would find, for example, that stars, dreams and sleep often occur in close proximity in the early poems.

To give an idea of how much a concordance can tell us about a poet's preoccupations, Parrish catalogues 'the extraordinary birds that beat, wheel, cry, hover, and keen through Yeats's poems': 8 hawks, 21 owls, 2 kites, 6 falcons, 15 eagles, 8 ospreys, 5 kingfishers, 2 robins, 2 gannets, 9 swallows, 3 water-hens, 2 water-fowls, 4 moorhens, 2 peahens, 3 moorfowl, 10 herons, 12 curlews, 3 bitterns, 6 gulls, 2 seagulls, 1 sea-mew, 10 doves, 1 ring-dove, 4 pigeons, 1 crane, 2 nightingales, 5 sparrows, 4 parrots, 2 crows, 11 cocks, 4 hens, 13 peacocks, 1 daw, 2 rooks, 1 stare, 1 nightjar, 2 lapwings, 1 jay, 1 cormorant, 1 grouse, 2 ducks, 16 swans, 6 ravens, 2 woodpeckers, 3 flamingos, 4 linnets, 2 snipe, 4 peewits, 8 geese, 1 barnacle-goose, 1 turkey and 6 cuckoos, 3 halcyons, 8 phoenix, and a single partridge (not in a pear tree). 'Bird' itself occurs 170 times, including compounds. For some reason, Parrish numbers 6 bats among the birds of prey. His list is equally extensive for animals.

Yeats's most frequently used word (apart from the two hundred commonest words which the *Concordance* omits), is 'all' (1019 times), which tells us a lot about his desire to totalise experience, to include and incorporate. In 'An Irish Airman Foresees His Death', he has Major Robert Gregory say: 'I balanced all, brought all to mind', and this could be a description of what Yeats himself constantly sets out to do in his verse, whether he is reflecting on his past life, considering his vision of the universe, or commenting on Irish history. The whole order of things is what concerns him, and it is therefore no surprise that 'all' is his commonest word. It is nearly twice as frequent as the next commonest word, 'old'. Parrish finds the high incidence of this word surprising. Given that much of Yeats's later poetry is concerned with personal ageing, while his early poetry laments a world grown old, I don't find this so unexpected. On the contrary, Yeats is the poet *par excellence* of old age and all that it entails, extracting some of his most powerful drama out of 'this absurdity . . . / Decrepit age that has been tied to me / As to a dog's tail'.

We can learn much about Yeats's ideology, about his characteristic attitudes and assumptions about a whole range of topics, by examining the range and recurrence of the words he uses to define them. For example, by comparing the different words used to refer to women ('lady', 'girl', 'wench', etc.) with those used of men ('warrior', 'hero', 'fellow', etc.) we can form a revealing profile of Yeats's prevailing sexual ideology. One poem is significantly called 'The Hero, the Girl and the Fool': we might ask ourselves what sex we assume the last word to refer to. What is striking is that, though Yeats is the great poet of heterosexual love, and constantly returns to the theme of woman in his verse, 'man'/'men' outnumber 'woman'/'women' by 510/263 to 130/66, while 'he' outnumbers 'she' by 815 to 370. Men remain the dominant parties in this world, though, significantly, the 2:1 ratio drops when the female is in the object position as 'her'. (NB, though, that 'her' is both pronoun and adjective, corresponding to both 'him' and 'his'.) Yeats's pronouns tell you that a woman's place is at the receiving end of a sentence. When we bear in mind that, except in some of the dramatic lyrics, the 'I' of these poems is masculine, the disparity is even more striking.

Yeats's pronouns are exceptionally revealing. As one might expect from his egocentric stance, 'I' occurs 2265 times, almost as frequently as the indefinite article, whereas 'me' occurs only 464 times. Yeats is much more at home when he is in the subject position of the verb, the actor and doer, the addresser, rather than the acted-upon and addressed. Although as a pronoun it corresponds to both 'I' and 'me', 'you' (including 65 'ye', 68 'thee' and 107 'thou') occurs only 985 times. The proud and solitary Yeats overwhelms the others in his poetry, and he is much more inclined to say 'I' than to say 'we' (472) or 'us' (174).

It is not only the most frequent words that can tell us about a poet's style. As much can be learnt by looking at the words he uses only once. These are known as *nonce words*, or more technically, *hapax legomena*. The editor of the *Concordance* points out for example that in the opening stanza of 'Byzantium', out of a total of 43 different words, Yeats uses nine words which occur nowhere else in his verse, and five more which show up elsewhere only once or twice. (The words are, respectively, 'unpurged', 'recede', 'Emperor', 'resonance', 'recedes', 'night-walkers', 'cathedral', 'disdains', 'complexities'; and 'abed', 'soldiery', 'gong', 'starlit', 'dome'.) The effect of this is to make the poem verbally quite unusual set against the general body of his work. Linguistically, it breaks new ground, defining a different kind of *verbal universe* from that to which we are accustomed in his work.

There are in fact a considerable number of nonce words in Yeats's work. They are very frequently unexpected and powerful images, which interrupt the smooth movement of the syntax with a kind of shock. Even when used more than once, the rarity of a word can bring a shock of surprise when it does appear in a poet's work, particularly when used in quite different ways. Take the example already referred to briefly above, the word 'delirium', in 'September 1913', which occurs only once elsewhere in his work (in 'The Tower' he speaks of 'testy delirium', a more conventional usage). In 'September 1913', 'All that delirium of the brave' is a startling expression. We wouldn't normally expect 'delirium' to be applied to bravery, so that we have to pause to think what it can possibly mean in the context. But, on reflection, it's a highly apposite word, recalling, for example, those Celtic warriors who went into battle in a kind of trance which enabled them to suffer the most appalling wounds apparently without noticing. It suggests, too, that the bravery, although undeniably heroic, has an edge of madness to it, but also that that madness might be part of its intoxicating attraction. As with the 'terrible beauty' of the poem 'Easter 1916', 'excess of love' may have 'Bewildered them till they died'. But the admiration contained in the expression also implies that being 'enchanted to a stone' was a positive transformation, the loss of which is now to be regretted. Thus, the rarity of the word 'delirium' itself testifies to the distinguished and exceptional nature of the experience which it sums up. This kind of thing is rare in the world of history, yet had become so commonplace in the nationalist movement as to seem a contagion.

Concordances usually do not list the occurrence of the two hundred or so commonest words in the language – apart from the pronouns, by and large those little words which have no specific meaning in themselves but function as grammatical *connectives*, 'a' and 'the', 'of' and 'and', 'which' and 'that', 'by', 'with' and 'from', and so on. Nevertheless, we can learn a lot from looking at the *frequency* of their occurrence in a poet's work, for the ratio with which particular connectives will occur differs considerably from poet to poet. As we have seen with his pronouns, by looking at how frequently the poet uses these basic units of speech, we can learn a great deal not only about his style but also about his ideology, about how he perceives the world. Take, for example, the definite or indefinite article and similar parts of speech. Yeats uses 'the' three times more frequently than 'a' (8436/2841 times). This ratio may correspond to the normal ratio of the articles in everyday use, or may diverge considerably from it. We can assess whether Yeats's usage is unusual either by testing the ratio of 'the' to 'a' in passages randomly selected from a range of other texts (which might involve considerable work with a computer) or by comparing it with the ratio of definite and indefinite articles in the work of other poets for whom a concordance already exists, such as John Milton or Gerard Manley Hopkins. This statistical analysis may lead us to draw certain conclusions about Yeats's style in general. More impressionistically, however, we may be alerted to the way in which the tone of a passage can be subtly altered by a paced alternation of these articles or their absence.

The opening of 'Coole Park, 1929' adds pathos to the image of noble decline it presents by starting with the indeterminacy of a series of indefinite articles, before moving to a more specific and demonstrative 'that' which seems to point at a particular time and place:

> I meditate upon a swallow's flight,
> Upon an aged woman and her house,
> A sycamore and lime tree lost in night
> Although that western cloud is luminous.

The change to 'that' dramatically transforms the indefinite articles which precede it: from meaning *any* swallow, any aged woman, house, sycamore or lime it implies *this particular* bird, woman, house, tree, which we know is one of many but which is nevertheless special. The two indefinite articles which close the stanza then become totalities which unify diversity into singleness, something achieved between *those* particular walls and no others: 'Thoughts long knitted into a single thought, / A dance-like glory that those walls begot'.

Whether articles or adjectives, these little words which precede a noun ('a' and 'the', 'this' and 'that', 'these' and 'those', 'all' and 'any') fulfil a similar function, and Yeats is skilful in achieving maximum effect from their permutation and interplay.

Sometimes the omission of such a grammatical qualifier can have an effect of its own, as in the way 'Great works', 'scholars', 'poets' and 'Thoughts' take on an authoritative general status in this stanza. When 'Two Songs from a Play' begin 'I saw a staring virgin stand / Where holy Dionysus died', the indefinite article makes an important point. This is not *the* archetypal semi-divine virgin, the Virgin Mary, mother of Christ, but another mother of another god, Semele mother of Dionysus, one of many who are then implicitly seen as prefiguring Mary and her son. The last line of the stanza, however, 'As though God's death were but a play', sets up the tension between a single God, without any article at all (neither 'a' nor 'the' God) and the idea of *a* play, again one of many in the cycles of death and resurrection through which that God passes. The God is one, but dies many times in many different forms in play after play. The second stanza spells this out, using 'Another' three times at the beginning of the line to propose a repetition of this mythological divine cycle, before coming to the new incarnation. Now, *a* staring virgin' becomes '*that* fierce virgin', as if to emphasise a greater knowledge and involvement on our part, since this incarnation is one in whose shadow we still live.

Yeats is in fact very fond of the demonstrative adjective, particularly 'that' – 'that enquiring man John Synge', 'All *that* delirium of the brave', and so on. Altogether, 'that' occurs 2397 times in his poetry, though our calculation is complicated by the fact that the word can be either adjective or pronoun or conjunction (= 'which'), and the *Concordance* does not distinguish the three usages. The device can allow for dramatic effect, as for example in 'Solomon and the Witch', which begins abruptly 'And thus declared that Arab lady' as if we should know her already, plunging us into her story before we can ask 'Which Arab lady?' By listening, it is implied, we will find out. The demonstrative pronoun functions in a similar way in '*That* is no country for old men', giving a great deal of emphasis to the beginning of 'Sailing to Byzantium' (as opposed to saying, for example, 'It is no country for old men'). Not only does the abrupt opening suggest an explosion of fury, but 'That' rather than 'this' tells us that he has already turned his back on Ireland, already rejected it. The final couplet of this stanza confirms that he has already 'come / To the holy city of Byzantium'.

In 'Easter 1916', on the other hand, the repeated 'this', as Yeats lists the people who have taken part in the uprising, gives a feeling of intimacy and shared experience to the recitation, counteracting the fact that he does not mention their names by suggesting that it is unnecessary. We are all so much part of this shared communion that we know at once who is spoken of: 'This man had kept a school . . . / This other his helper and friend / . . . This other man I had dreamed . . .' Noticeably, the sequence begins with a 'that': 'That woman's days were spent / In ignorant good-will'. It is still more difficult for Yeats to admit intimacy with a woman such as Con Markiewicz, and more difficult to forgive her involvement in the world of shrill argument, than it is to accept John MacBride back into companionship, 'a drunken vainglorious lout' who took Maud Gonne away from him. The 'that', contrasted with the closer 'this', adds a dramatic tension to the list, because the person he knows best, most intimately, in this sequence, is precisely the one who is kept at greatest distance because of this intimacy. The company into which they enter is, after all, an *impersonal* one, which transcends petty personal affections and antipathies.

It should be clear that questions of vocabulary are not separable from those of *metaphor*. A poet can use a word in what seems like a straightforward, non-metaphorical sense, as in the opening to 'Sailing to Byzantium', where he speaks of 'the young / In one another's arms, birds in the trees', and so on. But even here the apparently literal references take on a representative status – the young, the birds, 'The salmon-falls, the mackerel-crowded seas' become symbols of the whole world of youth and sexual procreation, part *metaphor* and part *metonymy*. For if the salmon-falls become metaphors of the world of nature, always spawning and changing, forever on the move, they are also a literal *part* of that world, and therefore act as a metonymy, that is, a part which symbolises the whole from which it is drawn.

One could devote a whole book to Yeats's use of *metaphor*. Much that has been said under Themes and in the present section relates to this topic. What I wish to do here is to say a little about the general structure of his use of metaphor.

Yeats frequently employs metaphor most powerfully as an element in an *argument*. (It is, after all, out of 'the quarrel with ourselves' that we make poetry, according to Yeats.) In 'Parnell's

Funeral', for example, when he says 'All that was sung, / All that was said in Ireland is a lie / Bred out of the contagion of the throng', the metaphor of 'contagion' clinches the argument with its unexpected and vivid immediacy (even though it is a latinate word). The metaphor allows Yeats to assert a case as if he had already proved it (to his own satisfaction, he has). Frequently his argument progresses by calling up one of his recurrent symbols or images, and it draws on our knowledge of its occurrence elsewhere in his work. An example of this is that moment when 'The swan has leaped into the desolate heaven' in 'Nineteen Hundred and Nineteen', where the poet immediately turns the real event into an image with an apocalyptic meaning that can be spelt out, explaining the metaphoric undertow of 'desolate' in the process: 'That image can bring wildness, bring a rage / To end all things'.

Very often, although intensely visual, his language turns out to be not so much metaphoric, involving an implied comparison between one thing and another, as *imagistic*. At the end of 'Byzantium' he speaks of 'Those images that yet / Fresh images beget, / That dolphin-torn, that gong-tormented sea'. Although this last line is acutely visual, its three main items, dolphin, gong and sea are as much literal as metaphoric elements of the scene: the poem had begun with the cathedral gong ringing out over the sea, and had gone on to speak of the dolphins in the waters around Byzantium. Of course, dolphin and gong also 'stand for' something else – the vitality of the living animal, the majesty and authority of religion over the spirit, but they do this primarily as images. Direct metaphor is reduced to a subordinate position here, in the words 'torn' and 'tormented', since neither of them can literally be applied to water. The first very vividly catches the force with which the dolphin leaps from and returns to its elements. The second communicates the extent to which that element is troubled by the demands of the spiritual. In the same way, images do not really 'beget' images. Begetting is an activity of the world of nature, not art. To use the word here therefore reinforces the antithesis and the synthesis Yeats is making of the worlds of matter and spirit. But this larger metaphoric argument derives from the whole situation, and is embodied only in a subdued way in particular local metaphors. An earlier line, 'The fury and the mire of human veins', is more clearly metaphoric in a traditional sense, but it involves too the use of *metonymy*, the part for the whole, since 'veins' is being used to stand for the whole corporeal being of man and woman, symbolised by its most vital network, the blood stream, and its most vital fluid, blood. Metonymy is indeed a much more frequent device than metaphor in a poet who thinks in images. For in so far as images have a meaning beyond themselves they are not simply *metaphors for* but *metonymic instances of* that which they stand for. The veins are part of the very whole they represent, the human body. To see that highly organised system as 'fury' and 'mire' is to make some quite striking claims about the nature of the human. Yet instead of arguing his case theoretically, Yeats *embodies* it in an image. As we have seen already, Yeats believed that 'Man can embody truth but he cannot know it'. The way he uses metaphor and metonymy itself exemplifies this argument. They both directly embody 'truths' he could not persuade us of by theoretical argument after the manner of Hegel (see Chapter 3.12). In that sense, all Yeats's poems are like the Song of Sixpence. It is up to us to open the pie.

5

Commentary: 'Meru'

Civilisation is hooped together, brought
Under a rule, under the semblance of peace
By manifold illusion; but man's life is thought,
And he, despite his terror, cannot cease
Ravening through century after century,
Ravening, raging and uprooting that he may come
Into the desolation of reality:
Egypt and Greece, good-bye, and good-bye, Rome!

Hermits upon Mount Meru or Everest,
Caverned in night under the drifted snow,
Or where that snow and winter's dreadful blast
Beat down upon their naked bodies, know
That day brings round the night, that before dawn
His glory and his monuments are gone.

For such an expert and experimenter with poetic forms, Yeats
wrote few sonnets. His choice of the form here is therefore
significant. This is the traditional Shakespearean sonnet, in
which three pentameter quatrains, rhyming abab, are completed
by a final rhyming couplet. The argument is divided between
the octet (the first eight lines) and the sestet (the last six lines).
These function as separate units of sense: the main outline of
the argument is set out in the octet, and certain conclusions are
drawn and morals pointed in the sestet. The final couplet usually
functions as a fairly separate unit within this division. Here, it
sums up what the hermits 'know'.

The form makes possible, indeed encourages, a kind of
intellectual, argumentative or persuasive poetry in which a case
is presented, elaborated and then rounded off in the couplet,
which aims at clinching with an almost aphoristic force the logic,
or rhetoric, of the preceding argument. Yeats's poem is a
'thesis' poem of this kind, beginning with a proposition about

153

'civilisation' which is then amplified and illustrated. But what he does with the form is interesting.

The very compactness of the sonnet form, while it gives it aphoristic force, also tends to restrict its scope. It is customary for it to be the form for love poetry, usually of a rather formal kind, rather than for world-encompassing philosophical statements. It is for just this purpose, however, that Yeats deploys it here, and we feel at once an exhilarating clash between its tight, terse form and the millennia of history of which it speaks. The whole octet is a single sentence, yet within it several thousand years of human history are summed up and then, in the list of civilisations in the last line, casually dismissed. A thousand years, the poem suggests, pass as quickly as the wave of a hand, or as quickly as it takes a sonnet to be spoken. Yet that single sentence, like the subject of which it speaks, 'ravens' and 'rages' through the octet. The idea pushes its way through the poem as one verb of action succeeds another in the sweeping syntax upon which the octet tries to impose a semblance of rule.

The poem itself, one might say, is 'hooped together' by the rhyme scheme, but, as the frequent enjambements indicate, it strives to break out of its constraints, enacting the contradiction of which it speaks. Note, for example, how the enjambement of 'brought/Under' subverts the process it describes, breaking up the act of bringing under control by splitting verb from preposition. 'Manifold illusion' is foregrounded with equally subversive force in this way, reflecting back on the previous line to remind how much this is a mere *semblance* of peace, not the real thing.

The sense and sentence turn on that centrally placed 'but'. Although the qualifying 'despite his terror' retards the pace, as if holding off the enormity of what is now to be faced, the enjambement of 'cannot cease/Ravening' emphasises both verbs, and underlines the inexorability and violence of the process it describes. 'Ravening' is given added emphasis by its place at the beginning of the line (compare 'Beat down' in the sestet). This downgrades mere repetitive 'century after century' to secondary status, compared with the act of ravening. This is further stressed by being reiterated at the start of the next line. It is doubly reinforced by the alliterated verbs which expand on what this 'Ravening' means – 'raging' (internal feelings outwardly expressed) and 'uprooting' (external actions). These verbs not only expand, they also intensify the process, until that 'uprooting' brings us as readers 'Into the desolation of reality'. This last phrase has been the whole destination of the sentence, and it seems to offer a kind of peace and stability after the turbulent continuous present of the preceding verbs. Placing 'come' at the end of the line, like 'know' in the sestet, holds us back for an instant from the moment of truth. But because in each case we have waited so long for the sentence to reach its climax, we experience a sense of narrative relief and release when this desolation is revealed.

All that remains then, as if in a postscript, is to dismiss all those centuries of ravening and uprooting, hooping together and bringing under a rule with a wave of the hand. All civilisations, Yeats suggests, are both a process of destruction and a simultaneous bringing to order. In another poem in the sequence 'Supernatural Songs' from which 'Meru' comes, the Emperor Charlemagne is seen as emerging from the barbarian cultures that put an end to Rome. In the same way, Rome had previously conquered Greece and Egypt, and was itself, according to Virgil, the beneficiary of Troy's destruction.

Man invents illusions, man destroys them. Something in his nature drives him to uproot the very illusions he has created to protect himself from his terror. Thought itself seeks its own destruction. It is a condition of intellectual integrity, Yeats says in 'A Dialogue of Self and Soul', that 'I am content to follow to its source / Every event in action and in thought; / Measure the lot; forgive myself the lot!' Here, then, thought is not just a creative, 'progressive' force. It also tears down and destroys, discontented until it can stand face to face with a reality unobscured by ideological delusions, by faith or conviction or hope. This reality may be a 'desolation', but it is true, and therefore the only thing worth knowing and the only thing that can be truly known (since all else is deception). The poem is in fact endorsing the idea of extremism in the pursuit of truth.

The sestet deals with those who have already acquired this knowledge, as if to confirm by their precedent the argument put forward in the octet. There is an equally dramatic use of syntax and stanza here. The subject of the sentence is identified in the opening word. But the main verb ('know') is withheld until the end of the quatrain, delayed by the description of those hermits. The main sentence is 'Hermits . . . know'. This is amplified by detail which fills out our knowledge of who these hermits are, before we are told what they know. 'Caverned', though it describes how the hermits live, also calls up Plato's idea that the world we live in is a cave in which we see on the wall mere shadows cast by the reality outside. 'Drifted snow' and 'Beat down' contrast the physical exigency and unfreedom of their bodies with the freedom of their minds. Alliteration of such sounds as 'b' and 'd' and 'n' here is a major element in binding the sentence together musically and in representing the harshness of the environment, since 'b' and 'd' as plosive and dental sounds are not really softened by the nasal 'n'. The formula by which 'snow' is repeated and extended into 'winter's dreadful blast' enacts the overwhelming hostility of the environment, in contrast to the frailty of their 'naked bodies', which suggests that they are not now even 'caverned'. Looking back we see that the word itself might have been merely metaphorical, referring to 'night' as the cavern in which they shelter.

The verb 'know', placed at the line end, pauses before it hurls us forward into the couplet, which finally allows us to share the hermits' knowledge. What it tells us, however, really only repeats what we have already learned, not intellectually but dramatically, in the rhetorical gesture which concludes the octet. Yeats uses the most obvious of metaphors, the cycle of night and day, to sum up this apparently arcane knowledge. But this merely reinforces our sense of having been admitted to a great truth, and seems appropriate in context because of the imagery of night, snow and winter of the preceding lines.

The tension in the poem between the formality and constraint of the sonnet form and the ferocity of the message it contains is reflected too in the play between a latinate language of abstractions and an Anglo-Saxon vocabulary of violent action. 'Civilisation', 'semblance', 'Manifold illusion', 'monuments' contrast with 'Ravening', 'raging', 'uprooting', and 'drifted', 'blast', 'Beat'. Significantly, however, two key words to describe the human response are Latin in origin: 'terror' and 'desolation'. They both seem to bring a kind of 'peace' to the process of 'ravening'. Alliteration transforms the Latin concept of 'glory' into the final desolate word 'gone'. The poem starts with a Latin-derived word 'civilisation' and ends with an Anglo-Saxon one. The two together sum up the whole poem: 'civilisation gone'. This is one poem, however, which does not, thankfully, refer to *Maud* Gonne.

What we see in this poem is a powerful, compact exposition of the philosophy of history which Yeats derived from the German philosopher Friedrich Nietzsche, in which the Apollonian principle of order and rule struggles through century after century with the Dionysian principle of energy and destruction. But as readers we do not need to know this, any more than we need to know that Meru is a sacred mountain in Hindu philosophy. The poem supplies all we need to know, and in doing so it offers a knowledge learnt 'in the marrow-bone', something we acquire from the very rhythms and rhetorical pace of the language.

Nevertheless, although 'Meru' can be understood on its own, with a minimum of external reference, it was originally published as the twelfth and last poem of the sequence 'Supernatural Songs', in the 1935 volume *A Full Moon in March*. Yeats there clearly intended the poem to be the culmination of an extended argument, in what is a very argumentative volume. (The book begins with 'Parnell's Funeral' and also contains 'Three Songs to the Same Tune' and 'A Prayer for Old Age'.) I have discussed other poems from the sequence in Chapter 3.16, and students should consider whether the readings there in any way modify and extend the interpretation offered here. Similarly, the discussion of Yeats's vision of history in Chapter 3.17 is highly pertinent to this poem. The simple and easily accessible idea of cyclical recurrence in the poem takes on a new and extended significance when set against the philosophy of history adumbrated in *A Vision*, or in Yeats's comments on 'Parnell's Funeral' (which can be found in Richard Finneran's notes to the new edition of the poems: see Guide to Further Reading, Section 1).

A knowledge of Yeats's political and other attitudes in the early 1930s will also have some effect on the way we read the poem (see Chapter 2.6). To return the poem to the historical context in which it was written can often substantially alter our perception of it. The image of 'our master Caesar' saving 'civilisation' in 'Long-Legged Fly', for example, takes on quite a new significance when we realise that 'Caesar' was in the 1930s an epithet frequently applied by their followers to the fascist dictators, who were often claimed to be saving civilisation from the Bolsheviks. When we realise that Yeats's poem was written while General Franco was waging the battle of Teruel, a turning point for the fascist powers in the Spanish Civil War, we might take a more sceptical view of Yeats's admiration for Caesar here. The changing contexts in which a poem is published, as Hugh Kenner has demonstrated in 'The Sacred Book of the Arts', can also radically affect our reading of it. While, then, a Yeats poem can often be read in isolation, there is much that we can add to our understanding of it by widening our knowledge of its biographical, literary and historical contexts.

W. B. Yeats: A Life and Times

Readers should be alerted to the fact that there are some disparities of dates between the chronologies of Yeats's life in some of the books listed in the Guide to Further Reading.

1858   Irish Republican Brotherhood founded.

1865   13 June, William Butler Yeats born at Georgeville, Sandymount Avenue, in Dublin, son of John Butler Yeats and Susan Yeats (née Pollexfen).

1867   Family moves to London (23 Fitzroy Road, Regent's Park), so that father can follow a career as a portrait painter. Brothers Robert and Jack and sister Elizabeth born here.
The Fenian Rising and execution of the 'Manchester Martyrs'.

1872   Yeats spends an extended holiday with maternal grandparents at Sligo in West of Ireland.

1873   Founding of the Home Rule League.

1874   Family moves to 14 Edith Villas, West Kensington.

1876   Family moves to 8 Woodstock Road, Bedford Park, Chiswick.

1877–80 Yeats attends Godolphin School, Hammersmith, London. Holidays in Sligo.

1877   Charles Stewart Parnell chairman of the Home Rule League.

1879   Irish Land League founded by Parnell and Michael Davitt.

1880–1   A decline in J. B. Yeats's income because of the Irish Land War sends the family back to Ireland (Balscadden Cottage, Howth, County Dublin), while he remains in London.

1881–3   Yeats attends Erasmus Smith High School, Harcourt St, Dublin

1882   Family moves to Island View, Howth. Yeats spends holidays with uncle George Pollexfen, Sligo. Writes first poems. Adolescent passion for his cousin Laura Armstrong.

Phoenix Park Murders. Land League suppressed.

1884   Refuses to go to Trinity College, Dublin. Attends instead the Metropolitan School of Art, Dublin. Family moves to Ashfield Terrace, Harold's Cross Road, Dublin.

1885   Two poems in *Dublin University Review*, March. Helps to fund Dublin Hermetic Society. Befriends Katherine Tynan and John O'Leary, the nationalist leader.

1886   Abandons art studies. Essays and reviews in Irish literary magazines. First séance. Begins to read Irish poets and Gaelic sagas.

Parnell allies with Gladstone on Home Rule Bill. Riots in Belfast. Bill defeated in Parliament.

1887   Family returns to London (58 Eardley Crescent, Earl's Court). Mother suffers two strokes. Yeats joins the Blavatsky Lodge of the London Theosophical Society. Visits William Morris. First poems in English magazines. Becomes literary correspondent for American newspapers, *Providence Sunday Journal* and *Boston Pilot*. Works in Bodleian Library, Oxford.

1888   Family moves to 3 Blenheim Terrace, Bedford Park, London. Last of the family land in Ireland sold under the terms of the Ashbourne Land Act. Meets Oscar Wilde, G. B. Shaw, W. E. Henley. Edits *Fairy and Folk Tales of the Irish Peasantry*.

1889   *The Wanderings of Oisin, and Other Poems*. Suffers a nervous collapse. Begins study of Blake's Prophetic Books. Meets and falls in love with Maud Gonne.

1890   Initiated into Hermetic Order of the Golden Dawn. Asked to leave Theosophists. Meets Florence Farr. Parnell's divorce case.

1891   Novel, *John Sherman and Dhoya*. *Representative Irish Tales*. Founding member of the Rhymers' Club and the London Irish Literary Society. Proposes marriage to Maud Gonne. Parnell dies and Gonne accompanies his body back from France. Yeats writes poem on Parnell. Founds National Literary Society in Dublin with O'Leary as president.

1892   *The Countess Kathleen and Various Legends and Lyrics. Irish Fairy Tales.*

1893   *The Celtic Twilight.* Edits, with Edwin J. Ellis, *The Works of Wm Blake.*
Second Home Rule Bill defeated in House of Lords. Gaelic League founded. Oscar Wilde arrested and gaoled for homosexuality.

1894   *The Land of Heart's Desire.* Visits Paris, where he sees *Axël* performed; stays with MacGregor Mathers, and proposes to Maud Gonne. Meets Olivia Shakespear ('Diana Vernon') through her cousin Lionel Johnson. Revises early poetry for first collected volume.

1895   First collected *Poems.* Edits *A Book of Irish Verse.* Shares rooms with Arthur Symons, in the Temple, London.

1896   Moves to 18 Woburn Buildings; affair with 'Diana Vernon'. Meets Lady Gregory. Tours west of Ireland with Symons, visiting Aran Islands. Visits Paris with Symons to found an order of Celtic Mysteries and meets John Synge. Attends a performance of Jarry's *Ubu Roi.* Joins the Irish Republican Brotherhood and works to unite the various Irish political factions.

1897   *The Adoration of the Magi. The Secret Rose.* Spends summer at Coole Park. Collects folklore there.
Jubilee Riots in Dublin.

1898   With Maud Gonne tours Irish communities in England and Scotland, and enters into a 'spiritual marriage' with her. Conceives idea of an Irish Literary Theatre with Lady Gregory and Edward Martyn.

1899   *The Wind Among the Reeds* wins the *Academy* prize as the year's best poetry book. Again proposes marriage unsuccessfully to Maud Gonne in Paris. *The Countess Cathleen* performed in Dublin as part of a programme for Irish Literary Theatre.
Boer War leads to wave of British jingoism. *The United Irishman* newspaper founded by Arthur Griffith, supports the Boers. Yeats, Maud Gonne and Edward

	Martyn join him on the pro-Boer Transvaal Committee. John MacBride, Maud Gonne's future husband, fights on the side of the Boers.
1900	Yeats's mother dies. Further unsuccessful proposal to Maud Gonne. Head of London branch of the Order of the Golden Dawn. Leaves IRB.
1901	Further proposal to Maud Gonne. Cumann na nGaedhael begun by Griffith. Queen Victoria dies. Edward VII ascends throne.
1902	Family returns to Dublin. Sister Elizabeth starts Dun Emer Press (later Cuala Press). Meets James Joyce. President of newly founded Irish National Theatre Society. *Diarmuid and Grania* written with George Moore. *Cathleen ni Houlihan* performed in Dublin, with Maud Gonne in the title role. Boer war ends in British defeat.
1903	*In the Seven Woods. Ideas of Good and Evil.* In February, Maud marries Major John MacBride. Three of Yeats's plays performed by the Irish National Dramatic Society in London. Financially successful lecture tour of USA. The Wyndham Land Act.
1904	*The King's Threshold.* On Christmas Eve the first performance at the Abbey Theatre, with Yeats as producer–manager, includes *On Baile's Strand.*
1905	*The Shadowy Waters* produced in London. *Stories of Red Hanrahan.* Sinn Fein founded by Arthur Griffith.
1906	*Poems 1899–1905.* Becomes director of Abbey Theatre, with Lady Gregory and Synge. *Deirdre* performed, 26 November.
1907	'The Playboy Riots' at the Abbey over Synge's *The Playboy of the Western World.* Yeats defends him. Father leaves for New York. Yeats tours Italian Renaissance cities with Lady Gregory and her son Robert.
1908	*Collected Works* (eight volumes) – complete revision of early work. Meets Ezra Pound. Visits Maud Gonne in Paris.
1909	Synge dies. Yeats edits Synge's *Poems and Translations.*
1910	*The Green Helmet and Other Poems.* Awarded Civil List pension of £150, but imposes condition that he is not prevented from campaigning for Irish nationalism.

Resigns theatre management. Crisis in affair with Mabel Dickinson.

1911   *Plays for an Irish Theatre*. Meets Miss Georgie Hyde-Lees, whom he is later to marry, through Olivia Shakespear. Visits Paris with Lady Gregory.

1912   Visits USA with Abbey Theatre Company. Lectures at Harvard University on 'The Theatre of Beauty'. Meets Rabindranath Tagore, the Bengali poet and mystic. *The Cutting of An Agate*. Stays with Maud Gonne in Normandy.

Irish Labour Party founded by James Connolly and James Larkin.

1913   *Poems Written in Discouragement*. In the autumn lives with Pound, at Stone Cottage in Sussex, editing Fenollosa's translation of Japanese Noh plays.

Irish Volunteers founded. Dublin lock-out and strike, in which Maud Gonne works for Connolly and Larkin.

1914   *Responsibilities: Poems and a Play*. Finishes *Reveries*, the first part of *Autobiographies*. Lecture tour of USA.

Third Home Rule Bill passes through all its stages but deferred at last minute by outbreak of the Great War on 4 August.

1915   Spends winter of 1914–15 with Pound at Stone Cottage. Refuses knighthood. Death of Hugh Lane in the sinking of *Lusitania* leads to dispute over Lane's bequest of paintings to Dublin city.

1916   Again spends winter with Pound at Stone Cottage. *At the Hawk's Well* performed in London.

Easter Uprising. Execution of fifteen leaders, including Connolly, Pearse and John MacBride. Yeats again proposes marriage to Maud Gonne. Sir Roger Casement hanged for treason.

1917   *The Wild Swans at Coole*. Buys Norman Tower at Ballylee, near Coole. Proposes marriage (unsuccessfully) to Iseult Gonne, Maud's daughter. 20 October, marries Georgie Hyde-Lees. Her automatic writing begins.

1918   *Per Amica Silentia Lunae*. *The Only Jealousy of Emer*. Divides time between Oxford, Glendalough and Sligo. Stays at Coole to supervise restoration of tower, then at Maud Gonne's in Dublin.

Major Robert Gregory dies on active service. 11 November, war ends.

1918–21   'The Troubles', period of brutal suppression by the British, carried out by the Black and Tans.

1919   26 February, birth of daughter Anne Butler Yeats. Family moves to Ballylee.

First meeting of Dail Eireann, the provisional Irish government, not recognised by the British authorities.

1920   American lecture tour; then Oxford.

1921   *Michael Robartes and the Dancer. Four Plays for Dancers.* The family lives at Shillingford, Berkshire, and in August moves to Thame, Oxford. 22 August, a son, William Michael, born.

6 December, Anglo-Irish Treaty creates the Irish Free State, with the six Protestant counties of Ulster opting out.

1922–3   The Irish Civil War, during which Yeats supports the pro-Treaty government, under Griffith and then Cosgrave, and opposes the intransigents under de Valera.

1922   *The Trembling of the Veil.* Father dies in New York. Yeats buys 28 Merrion Square, Dublin. Appointed Senator in first Irish Senate (until 1928). D.Litt. from Trinity College, Dublin.

Publication of T. S. Eliot's *The Waste Land* and James Joyce's *Ulysses.*

January, Griffith elected President of the Irish Provisional Government; dies 12 August. Cosgrave succeeds him, 9 September.

22 August, Michael Collins, former military commander of the IRA, assassinated in an ambush by the IRA rebels.

Mussolini's March on Rome leads to the foundation of a Fascist state.

1923   Visits Stockholm to receive Nobel Prize for Literature. De Valera orders a Republican ceasefire.

1924   *Essays. The Cat and the Moon and Certain Poems.* Working on *A Vision.* High blood pressure. Holiday with wife in Sicily in November.

1925   February, visits Italy. May, Ballylee. Senate speech on divorce, 11 June. Completes first version of *A Vision* (published 1926).

1926   *Estrangement.* Translation of *Oedipus Rex* produced at Abbey Theatre. Chairman of Committee to advise Minister of Finance on a new coinage.
De Valera founds Fianna Fail party.

1927   Summer at Ballylee. Lung congestion and influenza in October lead to collapse. Convalescence in Algeciras, Seville, Cannes.
Kevin O'Higgins, Minister of Justice, assassinated.

1928   *The Tower.* Winter at Rapallo with Pound; summer in Dublin and Ballylee. End of term as Senator.

1929   *A Packet for Ezra Pound. The Winding Stair* (New York). *Fighting the Waves* performed in Dublin. Collapses in Rapallo from Maltese fever.
Censorship of Publications Act.

1930   *The Words Upon the Window-pane* produced at Abbey Theatre (published 1934).

1931   D.Litt. degree from Oxford University. Divides time between Dublin, Coole and Oxford.

1932   *Words for Music Perhaps and Other Poems.* Lady Gregory dies. Helps to found Irish Academy of Letters. Last US lecture tour. Yeats moves to final Irish home, 'Riversdale', Rathfarnham, Dublin.
De Valera elected to office as head of a Fianna Fail government.

1933   *The Winding Stair and Other Poems. Collected Poems.* Honorary degree from Cambridge University. Yeats interested in and writing for O'Duffy's Irish Fascists, the Blueshirts. Hitler comes to power in Germany.

1934   *Wheels and Butterflies. Collected Plays. The King of the Great Clock Tower.* Steinach operation for sexual rejuvenation. Yeats convinced of its success. Rapallo and Rome.

1935   *A Full Moon in March. Dramatis Personae.* Translating *Upanishads.* Meets Lady Dorothy Wellesley.

1936   Seriously ill with heart problems and nephritis. Convalesces in Majorca, with *Upanishads* collaborator, Swami Shri Purohit. BBC lecture on 'Modern Poetry'. Dublin in June. *The Oxford Book of Modern Verse.*

IRA declared illegal by de Valera's government.

The Spanish Civil War begins with General Franco's military insurrection against the democratically elected government. (Franco victorious in 1939.)

1937   *A Speech and Two Poems.* Revised version of *A Vision.* *Essays 1931–1936.* Yeats gives four BBC broadcasts. Elected member of a London Club, the Athenaeum. Goes for winter to Menton and Cap Martin in the South of France.

New Irish constitution abandons dominion status.

1938   *The Herne's Egg and Other Plays. New Poems.* Stays with Dorothy Wellesley and Edith Heald. In August appears in public for the last time at the Abbey Theatre for the first performance of *Purgatory.* Works on *The Death of Cuchulain.* In the late summer Maud Gonne visits him at Riversdale.

Anglo-Irish agreement settles most outstanding disputes, April. De Valera re-elected, June.

Hitler occupies Austria, March. In September, Britain and France recognise at Munich his seizure of Czech Sudetenland.

1939   28 January, dies in France; buried at Roquebrune, France. (In 1948 reinterred in Drumcliff Churchyard, Sligo, as he wished.) *Last Poems and Two Plays* and *On the Boiler* published posthumously.

1 September, Hitler invades Poland. Second World War begins.

A Guide to Further Reading

1 YEATS'S TEXTS

For the authoritative text of a poem the student should consult *The Variorum Edition of the Poems of W. B. Yeats*, ed. Peter Allt and Russell K. Alspach (Macmillan, 1977). This brings together all the various versions of the poems printed in Yeats's lifetime in books and journals, starting with *The Dublin University Review* in 1885 and ending with the 1949 definitive edition of the *Collected Poems*, which Yeats approved shortly before his death. Much can be learnt about Yeats's methods of revision from this compilation.

The most complete edition for ordinary purposes is the paperback version of *The Poems: A New Edition*, ed. Richard J. Finneran (Macmillan, 1984), which includes 125 poems not contained in *The Collected Poems of W. B. Yeats* (Macmillan, 1933). Paperback selections include *W. B. Yeats: Selected Poetry and Prose* (Routledge, 1989), which has a valuable introduction and notes by Graham Martin, and *W. B. Yeats: Selected Poetry*, ed. A. Norman Jeffares (Pan/Macmillan, 1966).

Poems of W. B. Yeats: A New Selection, also selected and introduced by Jeffares (Macmillan, 1984) is a different selection. It rearranges the poems into a number of rather arbitrary sections, sometimes separating poems which make most sense when read in the conjunction Yeats gave them. Thus, 'Meditations in Time of Civil War' is placed under 'Moods and Meditations', thereby separating it from its close companion 'The Tower' (in the section 'Anglo-Irish Attitudes') and yet not linking it with its most obvious parallel, 'Easter 1916' (in the section 'Politics and Polemics'). The section titles, as can be seen, may give a misleading impression of what to expect from a poem. The selection has, however, a copious and invaluable range of notes on the poems (including a glossary of Irish people and places) largely drawn from the same author's essential source-book *A New Commentary on the Poems of W. B. Yeats* (Macmillan, 1984).

Jeffares has also edited and introduced the paperback *W. B. Yeats: Selected Criticism and Prose* (Pan/Macmillan, 1980). This is the collection referred to throughout my text as *C*.

Macmillan have published most of Yeats's prose, and some of this is now available in paperback, in particular *A Vision* (1981) and *Autobiographies* (1980). Both these are essential books for understanding Yeats's ideas and times. A less guarded version of his life can be obtained from the posthumously published first draft of the Autobiography, *Memoirs*, edited by Denis Donoghue (1988).

Other important collections of essays are *Explorations* (1962), *Mythologies* (1962) and *Essays and Introductions* (1961). Some of the early and rather mannered fiction is now available in paperback as *The Secret Rose and other Stories* (1982). This work is less interesting than his biographical and critical essays, which not only throw light on his poetry, but are worth reading for their own sake, being some of the most consummate prose written in this century. Not enough attention has yet been paid to Yeats's achievement as a prose stylist.

The two large volumes of *Uncollected Prose*, edited by John P. Frayne and Colton Johnson (Macmillan, 1975), collate the poet's extensive journalism, lectures and other miscellaneous prose. Judicious reading here can provide considerable insight into the poetry written at the same time. There is a comprehensive selection of *The Letters of W. B. Yeats* edited by Allan Wade (Macmillan, 1954). Oxford University Press are now producing a complete edition of the letters in several volumes, but so far only volume I (1865–95) has appeared.

A full account of Yeats's oeuvre is provided by Allan Wade, *A Bibliography of the Writings of W. B. Yeats* (Rupert Hart-Davis, 1968).

Jon Stallworthy's two books, *Between the Lines: Yeats's Poetry in the Making* and *Vision and Revision in Yeats's Last Poems* (Oxford University Press, 1965 and 1969), and Curtis Bradford's *Yeats at Work* (Southern Illinois University Press, 1965) contain and comment on successive manuscript drafts of many of the poems, and reveal a great deal both about his methods of composition and about the often completely different finished versions.

Finally, an indispensable aid to the study of the poetry is *A Concordance to the Poems of W. B. Yeats*, ed. Stephen Maxfield Parrish (Cornell University Press, 1963) – a checklist of all the words used in Yeats's poetry, and where they occur, which no library should be without.

2 BIOGRAPHICAL, HISTORICAL AND CULTURAL CONTEXTS

The standard biography is now almost half a century old, *W. B. Yeats 1865–1939*, first published in 1943 shortly after the poet's death by his friend Joseph Hone (Penguin Books, 1971). See also A. Norman Jeffares, *W. B. Yeats: Man and Poet* (Routledge & Kegan Paul, 1962). It is clearly time for a new biography that would incorporate all the material uncovered in the last two decades. The two books by Richard Ellmann, *Yeats: The Man and the Masks* (Faber & Faber, 1961), and *The Identity of Yeats* (Faber & Faber, 1954), combine biography and criticism to provide an informative introduction to the poet and his ideas. Of considerable use to students is Tim Prentki and Suheil Bushrui, *The International Companion to the Poetry of W. B. Yeats* (Colin Smythe, 1987).

Valuable background histories include Terence Brown's *Ireland: A Social and Cultural History 1922–79* (Fontana Paperbacks, 1981), and F. S. L. Lyons' two books, *Ireland Since the Famine* (Collins, 1971), and *Culture and Anarchy in Ireland, 1890–1939* (Oxford University Press, 1979). A more general history is offered by Edward Norman, *A History of Modern Ireland 1800–1969* (Penguin Books, 1973). An invigorating up-to-date account of the cultural and political crises that lie behind Yeats's work is provided by David Cairns and Shaun Richards in *Writing Ireland: Colonialism, Nationalism and Culture* (Manchester University Press, 1988). A more leisurely and not always accurate narrative of the Irish Literary Renaissance is offered by Ulick O'Connor's *Celtic Dawn* (Black Swan, 1985).

The most recent and authoritative history is that by R. F.

Foster, now appointed as Yeats's official biographer, *Modern Ireland 1600–1972* (Allen Lane, 1988).

Two studies which address Anglo-Irish culture as it is represented in Yeats's work are Donald T. Torchiana, *W. B. Yeats and Georgian Ireland* (Northwestern University Press, 1966) and Phillip L. Marcus's largely historical *Yeats and the Beginning of the Irish Renaissance* (Cornell University Press, 1970). More directly literary is Peter Ure's *Yeats and Anglo-Irish Literature* (Liverpool University Press, 1974). Laurence O'Connor's *Lost Ireland* (Rainbow, Dublin, 1985) is a photographic record of Ireland at the turn of the century, with an introduction and commentary by Patrick Gallagher.

Frank Kermode's *Romantic Image* (Routledge, 1957) and Graham Hough's *The Last Romantics* (Methuen, 1949) consider Yeats's writing in the context of his Pre-Raphaelite and *fin de siècle* predecessors and contemporaries.

Recent studies which place Yeats in the context of literary Modernism include Cairns Craig's vigorous and perceptive *Yeats, Eliot, Pound and the Politics of Poetry* (Croom Helm, 1982); and C. K. Stead's *Pound, Yeats, Eliot and the Modernist Movement* (Macmillan, 1986). This is a sequel to Stead's succinct and lucid *The New Poetic: Yeats to Eliot* (Penguin, 1967) – an admirable book for students to begin with.

W. B. Yeats: The Critical Heritage, edited by A. N. Jeffares (Routledge & Kegan Paul, 1977) collects together a large selection of the reviews of Yeats's major volumes as they appeared, and is a valuable source book for contemporary attitudes towards Yeats.

3 CRITICAL SELECTIONS

The collections of essays edited by James Hall and Martin Steinman, *The Permanence of Yeats* (Collier, 1961) and by John Unterecker for the *Twentieth Century Views* series (Prentice-Hall, 1963) both contain now classic essays by leading critics of the 1940s and 50s. The latter volume includes Hugh Kenner's 'The Sacred Book of the Arts', also in Pritchard and Cullingford below.

Three by now standard centenary collections of new essays

appeared in 1965: A. N. Jeffares and K. G. W. Cross (eds), *In Excited Reverie: A Centenary Tribute to W. B. Yeats 1865–1939* (Macmillan); D. E. S. Maxwell and S. B. Bushrui (eds), *W. B. Yeats 1865–1965. Centenary Essays* (Ibadan University Press); and Denis Donoghue and J. R. Mulryne (eds), *An Honoured Guest: New Essays on W. B. Yeats* (Edward Arnold, 1965).

An extremely thorough selection is *W. B. Yeats: A Critical Anthology*, edited by William H. Pritchard (Penguin Books, 1972). Beside many contemporary comments on Yeats by fellow writers and critics, and excerpts from Yeats's own remarks on his writing, it contains classic essays on his work by a wide variety of eminent scholars and poets.

Jon Stallworthy's rather old-fashioned selection on the *Last Poems* (1968), in the Macmillan Casebook series, necessarily does not contain any of the recent interesting work on the later Yeats. *Yeats: Poems, 1919–1935* (1984), Elizabeth Cullingford's selection in the same series, is a lively one, but does not print work published later than 1974. Nevertheless, both volumes contain substantial essays from critics cited elsewhere in this list, and the Casebook series is presently being updated.

There is inevitably some overlap between most of these collections. For the mass of new criticism that has appeared in journals and books in the last decade or so, the reader should consult the selection of essays and reviews and the regular bibliographies which appear in the two annuals, *Yeats Annual*, ed. Warwick Gould (Macmillan), and *Yeats: An Annual of Critical and Textual Studies*, ed. Richard Finneran (UMI Research Press). More recent criticism, of a structuralist, deconstructive, Marxist and feminist kind, will be represented in the projected volume on Yeats in the Longman *Critical Reader* series.

4 GENERAL GUIDES TO THE POETRY

John Unterecker's *A Reader's Guide to W. B. Yeats* (Thames and Hudson, 1959) outlines some of Yeats's major themes before providing a poem-by-poem interpretation of each volume in turn. Jeffares' *New Commentary* (see above) does not provide interpretations, but it does elucidate obscurities, explain allusions and provide references to the prose, which is extensively quoted, and to the historical and intellectual sources of Yeats's work. Edward Malins's *A Preface to Yeats* (Longman, 1974) combines a well-illustrated account of the literary and historical background (including the main intellectual influences on Yeats's ideas) with the close reading of a representative selection of poems, and a reference section on people and places in the work.

5 STUDIES OF PARTICULAR ASPECTS

Studies of Yeats's style include Robert Beum's *The Poetic Art of William Butler Yeats* (Frederick Ungar, 1969) and Marjorie Perloff's *Rhyme and Meaning in the Poetry of Yeats* (Mouton, 1970). See also Joseph Adams, *Yeats and the Masks of Syntax* (Macmillan, 1984). There are valuable essays on this subject by, among others, Donald Davie and John Holloway in the Penguin selection and in each of the selections listed above.

Frank Hughes Murphy examines the quest for reconciliation in *Yeats's Early Poetry* (Louisiana State University Press, 1975); while Daniel Albright in *The Myth Against Myth* (Oxford University Press, 1972) takes for theme Yeats's imagination in old age. *Yeats, Coole Park and Ballylee* (Johns Hopkins University Press, 1974) by Daniel A. Harris explores Yeats's myths of place and the transformations of the country house poem as a vehicle for social comment. Peter Ure's *Towards a Mythology* (Russell & Russell, 1946) was an early attempt to investigate the philosophy of *A Vision* as it is embodied in the poetry. By contrast, Dudley Young's *Out of Ireland* (Carcanet, 1975) casts a sceptical and humane eye on Yeats's apocalyptic visions.

There are several studies of Yeats's relation to magic and the occult, including M. C. Flannery's *Yeats and Magic* (Colin Smythe, 1977) Frank Kinahan's *Yeats, Folklore, and Occultism* (Unwin Hyman, 1988) and the collection *Yeats and the Occult*, edited by George Mills Harper (Macmillan, 1975). As several of the essays in the latter volume suggest, magic is inseparable from Neo-Platonist philosophy in Yeats's work, and this has been discussed by F. A. C. Wilson in two books, *W. B. Yeats and Tradition* (Methuen, 1968), largely about the last plays and related poems, and *Yeats and Iconography* (Gollancz, 1960).

Kathleen Raine is more idiosyncratic in that she is herself a poet in the Neo-Platonic tradition which links Yeats with the Romantic poets Blake and Shelley. Her *Yeats the Initiate* (Allen & Unwin, 1986) collects many of her essays on the subject. Graham Hough's *The Mystery Religion of W. B. Yeats* (Harvester Press, 1984) is a rather more dispassionate and readable study. There is a valuable discussion of how Yeats deploys Neo-Platonism in his verse in Ronald Snukal's *High Talk: The Philosophical Poetry of W. B. Yeats* (Cambridge University Press, 1972).

The authoritative study of Yeats's debt to Romantic and Victorian poetry is Harold Bloom's *Yeats* (Oxford University Press, 1970), in which Bloom sets out his highly elaborate Freudian theory of literary influence. There is an exciting and powerful examination of Yeats's intertextuality in Patrick J. Keane's *Yeats's Interactions with Tradition* (University of Missouri Press, 1987), a major study, which examines Neo-Platonism, Romanticism, Nietzsche and many other formative contexts for the writing of Yeats's poems, in a wide-ranging and detailed examination of the verse. George Bornstein's two books, *Yeats and Shelley* and *Transformations of Romanticism in Yeats, Eliot and Stevens* (Chicago University Press, 1970 and 1976) are fruitful considerations of this inheritance.

The link between Neo-Platonism and art has been explored by, among others, George Melchiori, particularly in relation to the Italian Renaissance, in *The Whole Mystery of Art* (Routledge & Kegan Paul, 1960). Elizabeth Loizeaux's massively informative *Yeats and the Visual Arts* (Rutgers University Press, 1986) surveys the whole range of interartistic relations throughout Yeats's career.

Denis Donoghue's brief, somewhat baroque essay *Yeats* (Fontana, 1971), nevertheless provides a stimulating survey of the poet and is particularly interesting on Yeats's relation to Nietzsche. Otto Bohlmann's *Yeats and Nietzsche* (Macmillan, 1982) examines the influence in depth. There is a brilliant interpretation of Yeats's philosophy of historical doubling in Thomas R. Whitaker's *Swan and Shadow: Yeats's Dialogue with History* (University of North Carolina Press, 1964). Edward Engelberg, in *The Vast Design: Patterns in W. B. Yeats's Aesthetic* (University of Toronto Press, 1984) presents an original and convincing account of the paradigms underlying Yeats's visions of art and of history. Starting from Kenner's idea of the unity of Yeats's volumes, David Young's *Troubled Mirror: A Study of Yeats's 'The Tower'* (University of Iowa Press, 1987) is a fine account of how the various poems interact, and an invaluable and lucid introduction to Yeats's poetic method.

Vivacious, partisan essays on Yeats's politics by Yvor Winters, W. H. Auden, George Orwell and Conor Cruise O'Brien are included in the Penguin selection. Elizabeth Cullingford has tried to disprove the charge of Fascism and to establish Yeats as really a man of the centre, in a study which is well-documented and highly informative but ultimately, unconvincing, *Yeats, Ireland and Fascism* (Macmillan, 1980). Paul Scott Stanfield argues for the coherence and consistency of Yeats's politics and aesthetics in *Yeats and Politics in the 1930s* (Macmillan, 1988). Grattan Freyer widens this discussion in *W. B. Yeats and the Anti-Democratic Tradition* (Gill & Macmillan, 1982), as does Geoffrey Thurley's *The Turbulent Dream: Passion and Politics in the Poetry of W. B. Yeats* (University of Queensland Press, 1983). In a more particular mode, Alex Zwerdling, in *Yeats and the Heroic Ideal* (Peter Owen, 1966) considers the use Yeats made of history past and present; and Michael Steinman, in *Yeats's Heroic Figures* (Macmillan, 1983) examines Yeats's treatment of Wilde, Parnell, Swift and Casement as instances of how his poetry transforms history.

Index of Poems Discussed

Adam's Curse, 4, 81–2
After Long Silence, 99, 129, 131
All Soul's Night, 28
Among School Children, 5–7, 9, 48, 57, 60, 84–9, 99, 115, 118
Ancestral Houses, 21, 28, 64–5, 126–8
Are You Content? 25
At Algeciras, 120

Beautiful Lofty Things, 35, 72, 141
Beggar to Beggar Cried, 97
Blood and the Moon, 23, 52, 65–6
Bronze Head, A, 31, 51, 69, 80, 93–4, 102, 142–3
Byzantium, 3, 28, 60, 119, 131, 146, 151–2

Choice, The, 53–4
Chosen, 28
Circus Animals' Desertion, The, 29, 56, 77–8, 128
Coat, A, 39
Cold Heaven, The, 119, 123, 125–6
Coming of Wisdom with Time, The, 39–40
Coole Park and Ballylee, 1931, 62–4
Coole Park, 1929, 64, 148–9
Crazy Jane Grown Old Looks at the Dancers, 90
Crazy Jane poems, 25, 89–90, 132, 135
Crazy Jane Talks with the Bishop, 89–90
Cuchulain Comforted, 119, 141
Cuchulain Fights with the Sea, 32
Curse of Cromwell, The, 135

Death, 119
Delphic Oracle upon Plotinus, The, 119

Dialogue of Self and Soul, A, 28, 29, 65, 91, 119–20, 128, 130, 135, 155

Easter 1916, 12, 41–2, 51, 59, 65, 68, 79, 97, 123, 139–40, 147, 150
Ego Dominus Tuus, 135
Ephemera, 33

Fascination of What's Difficult, The, 12, 39
Fergus and the Druid, 32
Fisherman, The, 75–7
Friends, 136–7

Ghost of Roger Casement, The, 48
Gyres, The, 105–7, 123–4, 125

Her Vision in the Wood, 99–100
Hero, the Girl and the Fool, The, 146
High Talk, 141
Hosting of the Sidhe, The, 32

I am of Ireland, 132
Image from a Past Life, An, 111
In Memory of Eva Gore-Booth and Con Markiewicz, 99, 124, 133–4
In Memory of Major Robert Gregory, 28, 75, 78–9
Introductory Rhymes, 22, 25–6
Irish Airman Foresees His Death, An, 26–7, 78, 122–3, 145

Lake Isle of Innisfree, The, 33
Lapis Lazuli, 9, 52, 80, 106
Last Confession, A, 99
Leda and the Swan, 6, 57, 61, 113–14
Lines Written in Dejection, 56
Long-Legged Fly, 29, 115–18, 132, 142, 157–8

Mad as the Mist and Snow, 91, 132
Magi, The, 112
Man and the Echo, The, 12, 45, 106
Man who Dreamed of Fairyland, The, 33
Man Young and Old, A, 98
Mask, The, 96, 135
Meditations in Time of Civil War, 45–6, 64–5, 66, 98, 110, 111, 126–8, 129
Meru, 103, 153–8
Michael Robartes and the Dancer, 82–4, 141
Mountain Tomb, The, 29
Municipal Gallery Revisited, The, 26, 47–8, 52, 74, 125, 129

Never Give all the Heart, 92
Nineteen Hundred and Nineteen, 42–4, 55, 61–2, 96–7, 151
No Second Troy, 94–6, 115

O Do not Love too Long, 92
O'Rahilly, The, 41
Oedipus at Colonus, 57
On those that hated 'The Playboy of the Western World', 1907, 71–2

Parnell's Funeral, 12, 23, 75, 150–1, 157
Phases of the Moon, The, 28, 56, 65, 81, 107, 110, 135
Pilgrim, The, 131–2
Pity of Love, The, 91
Politics, 135
Prayer for My Daughter, A, 42, 82, 123, 143
Prayer for Old Age, A, 89, 157
Presences, 91–3, 142

Reconciliation, 94–6
Red Hanrahan's Song about Ireland, 33
Remorse for Intemperate Speech, 51

Ribh considers Christian Love insufficient, 101
Rose of the World, The, 115
Rose Tree, The, 41

Sad Shepherd, The, 31
Sailing to Byzantium, 2–3, 9, 28, 60, 69, 85, 98, 149, 150
Second Coming, The, 59, 61, 102, 104–5, 106, 112, 113, 138–9
September 1913, 40, 142, 147
Solomon and the Witch, 135, 149
Song of the Happy Shepherd, 30–1
Sorrow of Love, The, 91
Spur, The, 48, 97, 135
Statues, The, 41, 51, 79–80, 141
Stolen Child, The, 31, 34
Supernatural Songs, 101, 155, 157

Three Marching Songs, 49–51
Three Songs to the Same Tune, 157
To a Friend whose Work has come to Nothing, 71
To a Shade, 141
To a Wealthy Man who Promised a Second Subscription to the Dublin Municipal Gallery if it were proved the People wanted Pictures, 71
To a Young Beauty, 81–2
To Dorothy Wellesley, 139
To Ireland in the Coming Times, 29
To the Rose upon the Rood of Time, 2
Tower, The, 22–3, 55, 56, 62, 63, 66, 98, 104, 111, 130, 137–8, 140, 142, 147
Two Songs from a Play, 51, 79, 111–12, 115, 131, 149

Under Ben Bulben, 29, 53, 106, 128
Under Saturn, 26
Under the Moon, 124

Vacillation, 119–20

Wanderings of Oisin, The, 32–3
What Then? 47
Whence had they come? 101
White Birds, The, 31–2

Wild Old Wicked Man, The, 91,
  132–3
Wild Swans at Coole, The, 55
Woman Young and Old, A, 98–
  100
Words, 37

Index of Names

AE (George Russell), 27, 33, 35
Alexander the Great, 6, 86
Aristotle, 5–7, 86–7
Auden, W. H., 15–17, 51

Berkeley, George, 22, 65
Blake, William, 58, 89, 122
Blavatsky, Madame, 28
Bradford, Curtis, 2
Burke, Edmund, 22, 23, 65
Burns, Robert, 58–9

Caesar, 116–18, 157–8
Callimachus, 52
Charlemagne, 102, 155
Collins, Michael, 45
Connolly, James, 41
Cosgrave, William, 48
Cromwell, Oliver, 21
Cuchulain, 32, 59, 77, 80, 105, 140
Cullingford, Elizabeth, 51

Dante Alighieri, 118
Darwin, Charles, 7
Davitt, Michael, 24
De Valera, Eamonn, 13, 45, 48
Donne, John, 128
Dowden, Edward, 27
Dowson, Ernest, 36

Eagleton, Terry, 10–11
Eliot, T. S., 17–18, 19–20, 39
Elizabeth I, 21
Ellmann, Richard, 50
Emmet, Robert, 22, 23, 75
Empedocles, 106

Ferguson, Sir Samuel, 35
Finneran, Richard, 157
Fish, Stanley, 7, 17–18
Fitzgerald, Edward, 75
Franco, General, 14, 50
Frye, Northrop, 107

Gladstone, W. E., 24
Golden Dawn, The, 27–9
Goldsmith, Oliver, 22, 65
Gonne, Iseult, 40
Gonne, Maud, 12, 29, 34–40, 42,
    56, 60, 69, 72–3, 79, 82, 85–9,
    91, 92, 93, 94, 97, 111, 115, 136–
    8, 150, 157
Gore-Booth, Eva, 64, 133–4
Grattan, Henry, 22–3, 24
Gregory, Lady Augusta, 21, 35,
    37, 38, 43, 63–4, 72–3, 75, 136
Gregory, Major Robert, 21, 26, 74,
    75, 77, 78–9, 123, 145
Grierson, Herbert, 43–4, 128
Griffith, Arthur, 45, 72

Hanrahan, 32, 137–8
Hardy, Thomas, 26
Heaney, Seamus, 2, 4
Hegel, G. W. F., 85–6, 101, 152
Helen (of Troy), 88–9, 91, 107,
    110, 111, 113–18, 137, 142
Hitler, Adolf, 102
Homer, 111, 118
Hone, Joseph, 51
Hopkins, G. M., 148
Horton, W. T., 28
Hugo, Victor, 49
Hyde, Douglas, 35
Hyde-Lees, Georgie, 40, 104

Irish Land League, 23
Irish Republican Brotherhood, 23,
    35–7

James II, 25
Jarrell, Randall, 143–4
Johnson, Lionel, 36, 74, 78
Joyce, James, 39, 72

Kain, R. M., 40–1
Keats, John, 4

Kenner, Hugh, 57, 158
Kermode, Frank, 84
Kuhn, Thomas, 7

Lane, Sir Hugh, 38, 71
Leda, 85, 88–9, 102, 107, 114–15
Lloyd George, David, 44

MacBride, John, 38, 42, 79, 97, 150
MacNeice, Louis, 12–14, 21
Mallarmé, Stéphane, 37
Mangan, James Clarence, 35
Markiewicz, Constance, 42, 150
Marlowe, Christopher, 116
Martyn, Edward, 38
Mathers, MacGregor, 28
Michael Angelo (Michelangelo), 83, 116–18
Milton, John, 148
Morris, William, 72
Mussolini, Benito, 14, 102

Napoleon, 101–2
Neo-Platonism, 28, 35–6, 85–9, 111, 112, 118, 119–20
Newton, Sir Isaac, 121
Niamh, 32
Nietzsche, Friedrich, 9, 80, 109–10, 118, 157

O'Brien, Conor Cruise, 51
O'Connell, Daniel, 23, 67–8, 75
O'Duffy, Eoin, 14, 50–1
O'Grady, Standish, 35
O'Higgins, Terence, 77
O'Leary, John, 34, 35, 36, 72
O'Rahilly, The, 41
Oisin, 32, 77
Orwell, George, 14-15, 51

Parnell, Charles Stewart, 12, 22, 23–4, 51, 67–8, 75, 77, 141
Parrish, Stephen Maxfield, 144–5, 146
Pearse, Padraic, 41, 59, 80, 105
Plato, 5–7, 47, 85–9, 140, 156

Plotinus, 119, 140
Pollexfens, the, 24, 26, 78
Pound, Ezra, 34, 39
Pythagoras, 86–8

Rembrandt van Ryn, 18
Rosenkreutz, Christian, 29

Schliemann, Heinrich, 113
Shakespear, Olivia (Diana Vernon), 37, 50, 136
Shakespeare, William, 4, 9, 118, 123, 135, 139, 143, 153
Shaw, G. B., 13
Shelley, P. B., 59–60
Sidhe, the, 32–3
Sophocles, 118
Stalin, Joseph, 102
Stallworthy, Jon, 2
Stendhal, 30
Swift, Jonathan, 22, 52, 65
Swinburne, Algernon Charles, 50
Symons, Arthur, 37
Synge, John, 37, 38, 71–2, 75, 78, 149

Tone, Wolfe, 22, 41, 75
Tuatha de Danaan, 32–3
Tynan, Katharine, 11, 34

Unterecker, John, 2

Verlaine, Paul, 37
Veronese, Paolo, 83
Villiers de l'Isle-Adam, 37
Virgil, 116, 155

William of Orange, 25
Winters, Yvor, 8–9

Yeats, Rev. William Butler, 25
Yeats, Elizabeth, 35
Yeats, John Butler, 25, 72–3
Yeats, Rev. John, 22
Young Ireland, 23, 35, 36, 73

Look at :- 'Coole Park and Bally Lee'
'The Second Coming'

All refer
to bird
imagery.
{ A vision called Dove or Swan

The Tower